CORNISH
RIVIERA EXPRESS

FROM THE FOOTPLATE

CORNISH
RIVIERA EXPRESS

STEPHEN AUSTIN

IAN ALLAN
Publishing

First published 1997

ISBN 0 7110 2536 3

© Stephen Austin 1997

Published by Ian Allan Publishing

an imprint of Ian Allan Ltd, Terminal House, Station Approach, Shepperton, Surrey TW17 8AS.
Printed by Ian Allan Printing Ltd at its works at Coombelands in Runnymede, England.

Code: 9708/B1

Front cover: **No 6026** *King John* **on Fairwood Troughs with the down 'Cornish Riviera' in September 1957.** *B. J. Swain/Colour-Rail*

Rear cover, bottom: **No 6826** *Nannerth Grange* **crosses Liskeard Viaduct on 17 July 1960.** *R. C. Riley*

Rear cover, top: **No 6010** *King Charles I* **at Lavington in 1953.** *P. M. Alexander/Colour-Rail*

Half title: **The 3.30pm Paddington-Truro passes Tigley box in June 1939; engine No 6022** *King Edward III***.** *H. K. Harman*

Title page: **Nos 5934** *Kneller Hall* **and 6015** *King Richard III* **are approaching the tunnel on Dainton bank on 15 August 1957.** *A. C. Cawston*

Below: **The 'Cornish Riviera Limited' at its zenith in August 1935, on the sea wall between Teignmouth Old Quay and Shaldon Bridge. 'King' class engine No 6002** *King William IV* **is hauling one of the two new sets of 'Centenary' coaches, comprising a**

Contents

Brake Third, two Thirds, Third Diner, First Kitchen/Diner, Composite, Brake Third, Third and two Brake Composites. Most users of this classic view cut off the far right where a pannier tank is standing on the Quay siding. *Great Western Railway*

Introduction

This is an illustration in words and pictures of how an express train was worked from Paddington to Penzance in 1957, the last year when the train was hauled entirely by steam power. While I have tried to describe the details accurately, I must emphasise that it *is* an illustration, not a record, and the narrative which forms the framework does not refer to any actual event.

The words are derived largely from the Working Timetable and its Appendices, and for those I thank the nationalisation of British Railways, which caused these documents to become available, and the Public Record Office, which enables us to study them. The project would not have been possible without the work of many researchers before me, and some of the most valuable sources are listed below.

The pictures are mostly from the Ian Allan Library of photographs and I must thank all those who were there recording the scene in those days. The recent photographs of locomotive details were taken with the assistance of the Great Western Society and the East Somerset Railway, and I am especially grateful to them for the freedom of their footplates.

I would also like to thank the Bluebell Railway, the MNLPS, Mr C. Austin, Mr R. M. Casserley, Mr D. S. Fish, Mr H. Hobden, Mr R. C. Riley, Mr R. Sewell, Mr D. Steggles of Newton Abbot Library, Mr D. P. Williams, and above all my sister Mrs Janet Price.

Readers may notice a lack of references to that important character, the passenger. The fact is that from the footplate of a steam engine, one does not feel much connection to the rest of the train; not because of any feeling of superiority but just because the surroundings are so different.

I hope readers who are not familiar with the steam engine will not feel they are being excluded by 'jargon', but it was impractical to explain every technical term, otherwise the book would have been several times this size. It is rather intended to encourage you to find out more about this fascinating machine. The same must also apply to the countless knowledgeable types who will say 'What about the...?' There are so many other things we would like to mention, but there is not the space for them here.

Setting the Time

Our story is set in the summer of 1957 and is told in the present tense. References to events between then and now are described as in the future. So slip back 40 years, to another era of rail travel: I won't say sit back and enjoy it, for as you will see, you are going to be doing the hard work...

Bibliography

The 10.30 Limited:
    W. G. Chapman
Atlas of the Great Western Railway:
    R. A. Cooke
The Cornish Riviera:
    S. P. B. Mais
Cornwall:
    Robin Davidson
The Cornwall Railway:
    R. J. Woodfin
The Golden Age of the GWR:
    Tim Bryan
The GWR in West Cornwall:
    A. Bennett
Great Western Coaches:
    Michael Harris
Great Western Signalling:
    A. Vaughan
Great Western Steam:
    W. A. Tuplin
Historical Survey of Great Western Stations:
    C. R. Potts
Locomotive Management:
    Hodgson & Lake
Railway World Special — Cornish Riviera:
    Chris Leigh
Signal Box Diagrams of the Great Western Railway:
    G. A. Pryer
Wessex Waterway:
    K. R. Clew

Schedule : Cornish Riviera

m.ch	Train No	SAT 130 Special Load	SAT 133***	SUN
		10.30am	10.35am	10.30am
0.00	Paddington dep	10.30am	10.35am	10.30am
1.17	Westbourne Park	10.34	10.39	10.34
9.03	Southall	10.43	10.48$\frac{1}{2}$	10.43
18.33	Slough	10.52	10.57$\frac{1}{2}$	10.54
24.16	Maidenhead	10.58	11.3$\frac{1}{2}$	11.0
30.78	Twyford	11.5	11.10	11.7
35.75	Reading	11.11	11.16	11.13
53.04	Newbury	11.29$\frac{1}{2}$	11.37	11.34
66.30	Bedwyn	11.43	11.53	11.50
70.05	Savernake L. L.	11.47	11.57$\frac{1}{2}$	11.55
81.04	Patney	11.58	12.8pm	12.8pm
94.42	Heywood Road Jn	12.10pm	12.20	12.24
96.64	Fairwood Jn	12.12	12.22	12.27
100.04	Clink Road Jn	12.15$\frac{1}{2}$	12.25$\frac{1}{2}$	12.30$\frac{1}{2}$
102.22	Blatchbridge Jn	12.18	12.28	12.33
115.21	Castle Cary	12.31	12.41	12.49
142.55	Taunton	12.59	1.9	1.22
153.44	Whiteball Tunnel	1.14	1.24	1.37
172.17	Cowley Bridge Jn	1.32	1.44	1.56
173.36	Exeter St David's	1.34	1.46	1.58
184.01	Dawlish Warren	1.47$\frac{1}{2}$	1.58$\frac{1}{2}$	2.10$\frac{1}{2}$
193.51	Newton Abbot arr	2.0	2.12	2.24
	dep	2.7	2.17	2.28
194.59	Aller Jn	2.10	2.20	2.31
197.44	Dainton Siding	2.15	2.25	2.36
202.29	Totnes	2.22	2.32	2.43$\frac{1}{2}$
206.58	Rattery	2.32	2.42	2.53$\frac{1}{2}$
209.18	Brent	2.35	2.45	2.56$\frac{1}{2}$
218.65	Hemerdon	2.48	2.58	3.10
223.74	Lipson Jn	2.55	3.5	3.18
225.40	Plymouth NR	3.0	arr 3.10	3.23
			dep 3.19	3.32
226.05	Devonport Jn	3.2	3.21	3.34
229.15	Royal Albert Bridge	3.9	3.26	3.39
229.57	Saltash	3.11	3.28	3.41
243.22	Liskeard	3.30	3.48	4.1
252.33	Bodmin Road	3.44	4.2	4.15
260.17	Par	3.56	4.14	4.26
264.58	St Austell			4.34
279.14	Truro arr	4.24	4.44	4.56
	dep	4.33	4.52	5.4
279.67	Penwithers Jn	4.35	4.54	5.6
284.31	Chacewater	4.42	5.1	
288.20	Redruth			arr 5.21
				dep 5.24
291.69	Camborne	4.52	5.11	arr 5.31
				dep 5.34
294.30	Gwinear Road		arr 5.15	
			dep 5.20	
299.29	St Erth	arr 5.8	5.30	arr 5.45
		dep 5.15		5.49
303.52	St Ives	arr 5.35		
305.01	Penzance		arr 5.40	arr 6.0

Truro arr	4.24	
dep	4.40	Penzance portion detached from rear.
Penwithers Jn	4.42	
Chacewater	4.49	
Camborne	5.1	
St. Erth arr	5.11	
dep	5.14	
Penzance arr	5.25	

Setting the Scene

The Crew

You are a fireman in No 8 Link at the Old Oak Common locomotive depot of British Railways (Western Region). Your job is principally to be ready to take any train to any place, should the engine crew allocated to the duty be unavailable for any reason. You do not, however, spend all your time sitting waiting for something to happen; you also have booked turns which take you to every part of the railway normally covered by this depot at least once every three months, thus keeping your route knowledge refreshed and current.

It is a summer evening in the year 1957. Just as you are going off duty, a message comes into the office that the fireman booked for tomorrow's 10.30am Paddington-Penzance is sick. The list clerk therefore reallocates the fireman of the 10.35am Penzance to take his place, and when you sign off you are handed a note instructing you to book on at 8.38am, prepare the engine and work the 10.35am to Plymouth. You will return home the next day, probably working the 11.0am Penzance-Paddington.

You walk home, thinking that you will need your kit for lodging overnight, that you will miss cricket practice tomorrow, and that you will be firing an engine for over five hours without a break, on one of the hardest footplate jobs in the country.

It thus comes about that you leave home at a pleasant hour, when the summer sun is well up and your neighbours are also starting work in shops and factories. You can be excused for passing them with a bit of an independent air. You are a man in the prime of your days, alert, superbly fit, having made a grade which few of them could tackle; the footplate is more exacting in selection than the Army, as well you know from your experience of National Service. While they swelter in Acton or Park Royal, you are off

Below: **A companion, less well known, view of the 'Centenary' train on its up run, beside the Teign near Bishopsteignton. Locomotive No 6003** *King George IV. Great Western Railway*

into the country. You will be in command of a machine that is the cynosure of all eyes when you set out with the down relief 'Cornish Riviera Express'.

The Train

The Cornish Riviera was invented by the Great Western Railway. Just who coined the name is not known, but it could have been E. M. Bradley of the Publicity Department, who wrote the book with that title, first published in 1904. The theme of the book was that the climate of Cornwall was, especially during the winter, as clement and healthful as that of the South of Europe. Its origin was that, in the latter years of the 19th century, it was clear that the mining industry of Cornwall was in irreversible decline, and the railway company needed to develop new sources of business for itself and for the county. Its purpose was to persuade that portion of the populace who could afford holidays to take them in Cornwall.

At the same time a new through train from Paddington to Penzance was introduced, at first called the 'Riviera Express', then named the 'Cornish Riviera Limited' for its second summer. The down train ran nonstop from Paddington to Plymouth, which was the longest nonstop run in the world at the time. A trial run had been made the previous year, using a Royal Train carrying the Prince of Wales; a company with the presumption to rename part of England would naturally not baulk at using the Royal Family for its experiments.

On 1 July 1904 the first down service was hauled from Paddington to Plymouth by the French 4-4-2 No 102 *La France* and taken on to Penzance by 4-4-0 No 3418 *Paddington*. The up train is believed to have been worked by engines of the 'City' class. At that time the railway was markedly different from the route we know today: the train went via Bristol to Exeter and ran on a single track along the South Devon coast and over several sections in west Cornwall.

On 2 July 1906 it was switched to the new route from Reading to Taunton via Castle Cary, which cut 20 miles off the distance, but at 225 nonstop miles it still retained its record until 1927. That autumn it became a year-round service. In 1908 a new line from Saltash to St Germans was opened, eliminating five of Cornwall's famous timber viaducts. Doubling of the track proceeded in stages and the last section, from Redruth to Scorrier, was finished in 1931.

As the Great Western's crack train, the 'Cornish Riviera' always received the latest and best in engines and rolling stock. The 'Dreadnought' coaches of 1905 had bodies 70ft long and 9ft 6in wide, the largest ever used in Britain. The 70-footers of 1923 ran in fixed sets and employed 'Buckeye' automatic couplings. The 'Centenary' stock of 1935 were the most

Above: **The postwar 'Cornish Riviera Express' at the same place as the 1935 picture (see page 4), on 10 June 1949. The 13-coach train of 1938 stock is hauled by No 6027** *King Richard I.* **The main difference from the earlier view is the removal of the tennis courts but the houses and trees beyond are little changed.** *E. D. Bruton*

luxurious coaches ever constructed by a British railway company and were intended to make the 'Cornish Riviera' equivalent to a Pullman car train. The 'City' and 'Bulldog' engines were superseded in turn by 'Stars', 'Castles' and then 'Kings' east of Plymouth, and by 'Halls', 'Granges' and 'Counties' in Cornwall.

The company exuded such glorious self-confidence that it even permitted its public to refer to the train by its railwayman's nickname of 'the 10.30 Limited'. (A 'limited' train is one to which the operators are not allowed to add extra coaches if more passengers book than the train's standard formation can carry, so the number of passengers has to be limited.) 10.30am was the departure time from Paddington. Departure from Penzance was at 10.0am, and until World War 2 a quaint little ceremony was enacted on the station platform every morning. The Station Inspector would stand by the telegraph office, and on hearing the 10 o'clock time signal, which was sent down the telegraph line from Paddington, he would blow a horn, whereon the guard would start his train.

There has always been a quaint English vagueness about the train name. The Great Western generally kept to the word 'Limited', but when British Railways introduced a headboard to be carried on the engine, it read 'Cornish Riviera'. For the 1956 summer season new headboards reading 'Cornish Riviera Limited'

Left: **The down train running into Newton Abbot on 16 July 1956, crossing the River Teign between Hackney marshalling yard and the station. No 6024** *King Edward I* **heads the new BR Standard train set.** *R. C. Riley*

Below: **The scene at the west end of Newton Abbot station on 4 July 1959. The 10.35am Paddington-Penzance, now diesel-hauled by No D602, stopped in the down loop, where 'King' No 6018** *King Henry VI,* **which had brought down the 'Cornish Riviera Express', was attached to assist it over the South Devon banks. The 'King' is carrying the rack on which train reporting numbers are mounted; it fits on the smokebox door locking handles.** *D. S. Fish*

Left: **One of the freight trains which have to share the tracks with expresses, 40 wagons behind '2800' 2-8-0 No 3814, at Richings Park, about to pass Iver station, on 11 March 1961. Most of the load is scrap metal destined for the Welsh steelworks.** *M. Pope*

Right: **On the main line in the 1930s; a typically mixed bunch of coaches hauled by a 'Star' class engine passing Twyford East signalbox.** *Ian Allan Library/LPC*

were made, but shortly afterwards it was decided to adopt 'Cornish Riviera Express' as the name, and that appears in all the literature. 1957 has started with the carriage roof boards reading 'Express' and the engine headboard reading 'Limited'. Use of the headboard is a bit variable and it is never moved to the front of an assisting engine. On the other hand, there was a recent occasion when the 'King' class engine broke down on the last lap into London, and the crew thoughtfully took the board with them onto their substitute mount, which was a '5700' class pannier tank.

In those interwar holiday times the 'Limited' was lavish in its connections to the West Country resorts. When conveying coaches for Penzance, St Ives, Falmouth, Plymouth, Kingsbridge, Exeter, Ilfracombe, Minehead and Weymouth, it left and entered London made up with nine portions, also claimed to be a record at the time. In the down direction three portions were detached without stopping the main train, by that inconvenient and inherently hazardous device, the slip coach. Slip portions were dropped off the back of the train as it approached Westbury, Taunton and Exeter. On the busiest days the load would be expanded into three or four 'parts', separate trains running in procession at about a mile a minute, about five miles apart. An amusing feature of the operation was that for some years the Ilfracombe coach was conveyed from Barnstaple attached to the rear of its great rival, the Southern Railway's 'Atlantic Coast Express'.

During the war the railway, which managed to hang on to the name 'Great' through Government control and amalgamation, kept up the 'Cornish Riviera' title and decorations, and thus the only train which, like the Windmill, never

closed, moved seamlessly into the British Railways era. While it is true that there have been far more changes during its history than folklore would imply, it is also true that there is more of a sense of continuity to it than to most trains, and it has the aura of a solid, dependable institution.

The Schedule
The timetable of the 'Limited' has not changed to any extent in the 30 years since the introduction of the 'King' class engines. In 1904 the times of the down train were:
Reading 36min, Bristol Pylle Hill Junction 2hr, Exeter 3hr 15min, Plymouth 4hr 27min, Penzance 7hr.

In 1927 the train was speeded up to reach Plymouth in 4hr and Penzance in 6hr 25min. The fastest ever schedule was that of 1933, with 3hr 57min to Plymouth.

In 1957 the times of the down train are as follows:

Monday-Friday: Reading 36min, Exeter 2hr 44½min, Plymouth 4hr, Truro 5hr 33min, Penzance 6hr 25min.
Saturday: Reading 41min, Exeter 3hr 4min, Plymouth 4hr 30min, Truro 5hr 56min, Penzance 6hr 55min.
Sunday: Reading 43min, Exeter 3hr 28min, Plymouth 4hr 57min, Truro 6hr 26min, Penzance 7hr 30min.

On Saturday the major part of the train runs through to St Ives, while Penzance passengers travel in two to four coaches which are detached at Truro and taken forward seven minutes later.

The corresponding times (to London) for the up train, leaving Penzance at 10.0am Monday-Saturday and 9.45am Sunday, are as follows (listed in reverse order for ease of comparison):

Monday-Friday: Reading 38min, Exeter 2hr 57min, Plymouth 4hr 10min, Truro 5hr 47min, Penzance 6hr 40min.
Saturday: Reading 45min, Exeter 3hr 24min, Plymouth 4hr 50min, Truro 6hr 24min, Penzance 7hr 20min.
Sunday: Reading 48min, Exeter 3hr 39min, Plymouth 5hr 10min, Truro 6hr 51min, Penzance 7hr 45min.

Note how much slower the up run is than the down, and the weekend times than the weekday. The weekend schedules are stretched out to allow for both the heavier loads and the much greater number of trains running but even so, it is quite usual for Saturday trains to be delayed for up to 3hr on the way by traffic congestion.

The relief train, the 10.35am from Paddington, runs every Saturday and 'as required' on Monday to Friday. Its times are:

Monday-Friday: Reading 38min, Exeter 3hr, Plymouth 4hr 20min, Truro 5hr 54min, Penzance 6hr 48min.
Saturday: Reading 41min, Exeter 3hr 11min, Plymouth 4hr 35min, Truro 6hr 9min, Penzance 7hr 5min.

There is no relief train on Sundays, and no corresponding up relief, its place being taken on Saturdays by a 9.20am from St Ives. Incidentally, in the last winter timetable, the times, Saturday as well, were the same as the summer weekday times, and there was no 'Cornish Riviera' on Sundays.

Left: **The main building of Newton Abbot station, built in 1927, still unspoilt in 1961. There are posters under the canopy announcing day trips to Plymouth for five shillings, Paignton Zoo for five shillings, Exeter for 3s 3d and somewhere unknown for 44s.**
J. R. Besley

Below left: **The summit of Dainton Incline, at the west end of the 264yd tunnel. A permanent way gang stand at the tunnel mouth. Near the tunnel is an early fish-tailed distant signal, painted red in this pre-1927 view.**
Ian Allan Library/LPC

Centre right: **There is a wealth of nostalgic detail in this scene from the late 1950s, with the Saltash chain ferry about to cross the Tamar below the Royal Albert Bridge, carrying a variety of vehicles including a Hants & Sussex Motor Services Ltd coach. The train on the bridge consists of a variety of coaches including two 70-footers. And look at the great mass of spare naval power moored up the river.**
Studio St Ives Ltd

Right: **Brunel's incredible bridge over the River Thames at Maidenhead. The main arches are partially balanced by concrete filling in the side arches. This view shows the eastern half of the bridge, with a diesel multiple-unit crossing on 14 February 1970.** *C. T. Gifford*

Right: **Moorswater Viaduct, showing some of the abandoned piers of the former timber viaduct. No 4505, one of the 20 '4500s' which were the last engines built at Wolverhampton, comes down to Coombe Junction with a brake van on 31 August 1954.** *R. C. Riley*

Left: **Very few early structures survived the attentions of successive administrations, but here is one that did: the up platform shelter at Menheniot, not only intact but recently repaired, seen on 10 July 1994.** *SHA*

Below right: **Map of the Great Western Railway.** *Author's collection*

Let us now refer to the trains by their reporting numbers, as will all the staff who have to deal with them. They are:
'Cornish Riviera' Mon-Sat down 130, up 635 (no number on Sundays).
10.35am Mon-Fri down 131, Sat down 133.
These reporting numbers will appear frequently in this account.

Although the public timetable lists the trains as nonstop between Paddington and Plymouth (Truro for 130 Saturday), in fact they all stop at Newton Abbot to attach or detach a second engine. Not advertising the stop means that it need not take place in a platform, and on Saturdays 130 can stop beside Laira locomotive depot to change engines and crews. On winter timetable Saturdays 130 takes on two fresh engines and crews at Newton Abbot and the relieved engine then assists 131 through to Plymouth. Its crew are supposed to remove the headboard and the number 130 from their smokebox front, but sometimes they forget, confusing observers as to which train is which. On summer Saturdays this cannot be done, because the assisting engine has to go through to Truro and must therefore be of a type permitted to cross the Royal Albert Bridge. On weekdays, since 131 may or may not run, the train engines are booked to work through to Plymouth, with additional engines from Newton Abbot to Plymouth if required.

The WR management (like their GWR predecessors) are no slouches when it comes to paperwork, and there are masses of tables laying down the maximum permitted loads and standard running times for each class of engine with each class of train over each route. Class A (express passenger) trains are further subdivided into three timing groups, causing the Working Timetable to have stars scattered all over it.

Trains 131 and 133 are in the fastest category, with three stars, but 130 is marked 'Special Load', which means in practice that it is timed faster still. As for what is a special load, the maximum is 13 coaches, of which two are detached at Westbury for Weymouth. In any event, trains of more than 16 coaches are not normally accepted in Paddington station.

The Weymouth coaches form one of the few surviving 'slip' workings. They uncouple from the main train as it is approaching Heywood Road Junction, and are brought to a stand before reaching the junction. An engine leaves Westbury at 11.48am for the 5min run to the junction, attaches the coaches and at 12.10pm returns to Westbury, where it couples them to the 11.45am Chippenham-Weymouth stopping train. Train 131 conveys the slip coaches when it runs, in which case this manoeuvre takes place slightly later, but there is plenty of time to complete it before the Weymouth train leaves Westbury at 12.42pm.

Before leaving the topic of schedules, it is worth noting that as 130 and 131 head westward, they gradually draw further apart. By the time they reach Cullompton, their separation is deemed sufficient to allow another train to be inserted between them. This is the 12.10pm Taunton-Exeter stopping passenger, which is booked to wait at Cullompton from 12.48 to 1.6pm and then follow 130 down to Exeter, arriving there eight minutes before 131 is due to pass. Later on there are four other trains due to be slotted in similarly: the 3.0am Severn Tunnel Jn to Tavistock Jn freight runs between them from Dawlish Warren to Newton Abbot; the 1.47pm Newton Abbot to Plymouth passenger; the 1.20pm Tavistock Jn to Penzance freight from Doublebois to Par; and the 4.15pm Truro to Penzance passenger. In all there are eight places where a preceding train has to be turned off the main line shortly before 130 overtakes it. These obviously depend on precise working by all concerned and on nothing going wrong; indeed, the timings for interleaving fast and slow trains along the route are in many cases decidedly optimistic.

The Route

More than any other highway, this one is attributed to a single personality, Isambard Kingdom Brunel. He was the Engineer of the Great Western, Bristol & Exeter, South Devon, Cornwall and West Cornwall Railway companies, which between them constructed the line from Paddington to Penzance, but although his command of these great enterprises was incredibly close and detailed, it inevitably slackened with time. When he began work on the Great Western on 9 March 1833, he rode out of Bristol alone, but the final link, the Royal Albert Bridge, was built almost entirely under the supervision of his deputies and he was not present for its opening on 2 May 1859.

The original GWR, on which trains were running as far as Reading by March 1840, is celebrated for its stupendous earthworks and its achievement of easy gradients and wide curves. The southern section of the Bristol & Exeter, from Taunton over the Blackdown Hills, was a different proposition and includes inclines leading up to Whiteball Summit, graded at 1 in 80 on the north side and 1 in 115 on the south.

This part was opened on 1 May 1844 and that such gradients were accepted on a main line demonstrates the pace of locomotive development in the previous 10 years.

The South Devon differs again; after lying dead level along the coast from Exeter to Newton Abbot, it strikes off over the hills. By the time he laid out this route, Brunel had decided to use the atmospheric system of traction, nowadays derided as a piece of eccentricity when it should be acclaimed as the most advanced concept of its day. By using stationary engines it removed the biggest and heaviest load from the train, viz the locomotive engines, and also, Brunel thought, the limitation on the power that could be installed to drive the trains. The principle was absolutely right of course and is employed in virtually all new railway works today, the only difference being that we now have an adequate means of transmitting power from the stationary plant to the train — electricity, which was not available to engineers in 1847. With this system gradients appeared to be of little consequence, so the South Devon line was laid out accordingly. From Aller Junction to Dainton Tunnel the line rises 208ft on an average gradient of 1 in 57, but there are 155yd at 1 in 36 which, while by no means the steepest railway gradient in the country, is pretty severe. On the other side the descent to Totnes includes half a mile at 1 in 38 and another at 1 in 43. Continuing westward there follow pitches at 1 in 47 and 1 in 52 up to

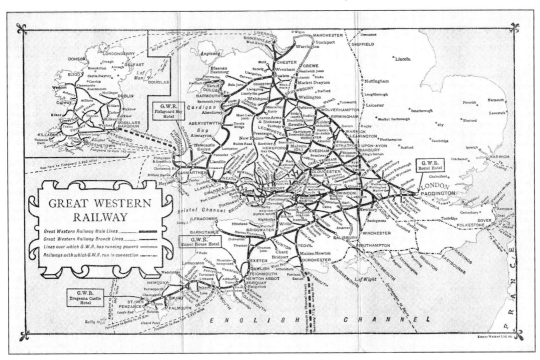

Tigley, 1 in 90 and 1 in 65 up to Rattery, easier grades to the highest point at Wrangaton, and an abrupt descent at 1 in 42 from Hemerdon down into Plymouth.

Faced with such hilly country, one might ask, why not continue along the coast? Besides the distance, there are the vastly indented estuaries of the Dart, Portle, Avon, Erme and Yealm which would be prohibitively expensive to cross; so, although Brunel would have sought easier gradients if he were designing the line for locomotive haulage, he would still have had to take to the foothills of Dartmoor.

West of Plymouth, that rocky country which looks so exciting when the sun shines, and so stark and bleak in bad weather, left the engineers no choice — although doubtless it seemed quite straightforward to the man who first surveyed a route, William Moorsom, who was responsible for the notorious Lickey Incline. In any case, massive works were out of the question. Both the Cornwall and West Cornwall companies were short of money throughout their short lives — although the Cornwall obtained its Act of Parliament in 1846, construction did not really begin until 1852. It intended to link Plymouth and Falmouth, but the portion between Truro and Falmouth was not completed until 1863 and has never risen above branch line status. The remainder was opened at the same time as the Royal Albert Bridge, which was its key feature and consumed nearly a fifth of its capital.

The first part of the 'Riviera' route to carry traffic was the Hayle Railway, opened to Redruth in December 1837. It was rebuilt and extended to become part of the West Cornwall Railway, opened from Penzance to Truro in August 1852. At that time the Truro terminus was at the river quay at Newham; when the Cornwall Railway arrived, an extension was made through Higher Town Tunnel to a new joint station. The West Cornwall line was built to the narrow gauge, but the Great Western, Bristol & Exeter and South Devon companies had, in return for contributing capital, obtained powers to oblige it to lay a broad gauge rail, which they invoked in 1864. This bankrupted the company, so it had no alternative to selling out to the Great Western. Only after that was broad gauge working established right through to Penzance and it only lasted for just over 25 years.

It is a slight exaggeration to say that there is no straight or level track between Aller Junction and Penzance, but only slight. There is a level mile across the Dart Valley at Totnes, some more at Plymouth, Menheniot and Redruth; the run in from Marazion to Penzance is level, and that is about the lot. The 1908 Saltash to St Germans deviation includes a long straight and a level

section, products of a later generation of construction with bigger money behind it. There can be no doubt that in this matter commerce's loss is our gain. Had there been, when the line was built, the resources to create a 'better' alignment, the result would have been a series of eyesores forming an outrage upon this supremely beautiful landscape. As it is, the way the line threads its way through hill and valley is an example of how business can be carried on without ruining the countryside, for others to note and copy.

The link from Reading to Taunton was assembled by joining up three secondary lines. The greater part, from Reading to Hungerford, was built in 1847 and extended to Devizes in 1862. The original line to Weymouth diverged from the London-Bristol main line near Chippenham and passed through Westbury and Yeovil, reaching the latter point by 1856. A branch line from Durston, near Taunton, to Yeovil was opened in 1853. To join them, only 29 miles of new construction were needed, from Patney to Westbury and from Castle Cary to Curry Rivel. The country was not difficult, the old lines were well aligned and the only severe gradients are on the climb over the Mendips between Frome and Castle Cary.

In 1933 the GWR took a leaf from the road-builders' book and provided Westbury and Frome with 'bypasses' which, lying well clear of the towns, are unique on the British railway system. The traveller on an express sees no towns of any size between Newbury and Taunton, and is clearly on a line whose sole purpose is to provide a fast transit between London and Exeter.

From the passenger's point of view, what makes this route so picturesque is the view from the window, and that is much enhanced by its plethora of viaducts. There are 66 of them, with a total length of 6 miles 816 yards. Half of them are, or were until they were rebuilt, Brunel's timber creations, whose story is well enough known. In their present form, those with arches and piers of the light-coloured local shale or granite are particularly beautiful additions to the Cornish landscape. Near London, the two most notable are Wharncliffe, with its massive brick arches standing in view of the Uxbridge Road, and Maidenhead, with its two 121ft spans across the Thames. Several generations have profited from Brunel's outrageous (for his time) idea of the weight and speed of trains which would use these structures, for they are still as built, flanked by extensions to the same designs added when the line was quadrupled in the 1890s.

The biggest conventional viaduct carries the line above the north of Truro's city centre. The

Right: **The original form of the 'King' class: No 6019** *King Henry V* **posed in front of the coal stage at Old Oak Common on 8 August 1928.** *E. R. Wethersett*

Below: **The final phase of the 'Kings', with enhanced superheater boiler and double chimney. The displacement lubrication system originally used was replaced by the mechanical pump seen on the side platform, to handle higher-temperature oil. A small but valuable addition was the speedometer gear by the rear coupled wheel. This is No 6006** *King George I,* **standing outside Swindon A Shop after her last overhaul on 10 June 1960.** *G. Wheeler*

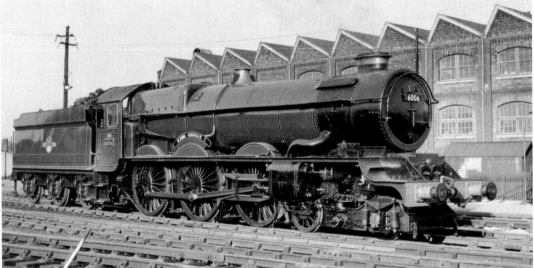

Right: **An express passing Lord Hills Bridge on its way out of Paddington in the late 1920s. The leading coach appears to be one of the first GWR dining cars, introduced in 1896. The engine, effulgent with polished metal and US bell, is of course the King of 'Kings', No 6000** *King George V.* *Ian Allan Library*

highest is St Pinnock, at 151ft; even in its modern form with steel girder spans, it presents a fantastic spectacle. The greatest of all is of course the Royal Albert Bridge at Saltash.

There is a human tendency to look back on one's youth as a time of stability, when the railways were solid and unchanging. In fact, this route has been in a state of constant change since the 'Riviera' began. In the decade before World War 1 the widening of the line was completed, Paddington station was enlarged and Exeter station was rebuilt. Much of what we see now was created with the aid of Government funding through the Loans and Guarantees Act of 1929. The Westbury and Frome bypasses, a new station at Taunton with quadrupling between Cogload Junction and Norton Fitzwarren, the last section of doubling in Cornwall and installation of Automatic Train Control on main routes were all products of this scheme, as were new office blocks and platform extensions at Paddington.

Now, all this historical stuff may be of interest to enthusiasts and tourists, but as a fireman you are only concerned with the tools you are given to do your job.

The Locomotives

The Great Western Railway's 'King' class has been lauded ever since 1927 as a triumph of locomotive engineering; and so it is, although not in the way the publicity has it. While it has been said that many a great idea is ruined by being handed to drawing office juniors, here the story is that of many engineers, having a basically unsound design foisted on them by seniors who should have known better, making it work by expending a great deal of worry and effort on various more or less satisfactory fixes. An ill-conceived combination of French and US practice with the head office's obsession with arbitrary statistics, has for 30 years hauled express trains as well as any engines have ever done, and that is their triumph.

Now, anyone with the temerity to criticise the Monarch of the Road will be asked what he means. There are three things wrong with it.

First, it is too big and heavy. The weight on each coupled axle is officially 22½ tons and, with additional gadgets bolted on over the years, is now probably more. It is only allowed to run on the Paddington to Plymouth, Cardiff and Wolverhampton main lines, and even on those it is restricted to main and relief lines, crossovers and adjacent refuge sidings in emergency, and is not normally permitted on goods lines. On the Plymouth route it is allowed into some of the goods loops, dead slow with great care.

Consequently, if a train normally 'King'-hauled is diverted to another route, a substitute engine has to be found.

Second, it was designed to make a claim to a nominal tractive effort of 40,000lb and in order to attain this, most of the dimensions of the 'Castle' class were changed slightly. The result is that many major and minor parts are different from the Great Western standards — the coupled wheels, for example, are 6ft 6in instead of the standard 6ft 8½in — and spares are peculiar to this class. This increased the cost of construction and maintenance, and makes a mockery of the standardisation which was the Great Western's great achievement in the early years of the century.

Below left: **Despite the increased tractive force provided by the 'Kings', they still needed assistance with maximum loads over the South Devon hills. This is 'Bulldog' No 3401** *Vancouver* **piloting the down 'Limited' in the 1930s.** *Ian Allan Library*

Below: **In the early part of 1956, when the 'Kings' were out of action with bogie problems, various engines were borrowed to take their place. This is LMSR 4-6-2 No 46210** *Lady Patricia* **on the down 'Limited' on 10 February, passing Stoneycombe Quarry halfway up Dainton bank.** *D.S. Fish*

Third, look at the cylinders. The layout is that of the French 4-cylinder compound 4-4-2s bought by the GWR in 1903, in which the connecting rods were made as short as possible. As a result the inside cylinders, driving the leading coupled axle, coincide with the front bogie wheels, and the outside cylinders, driving the second coupled axle, coincide with the rear bogie wheels, in both cases just where the main frame has to be cut away and there must be room for the bogie to pivot. The Swindon drawing office copied this, apparently without thought, and then piled error on error by placing the valve motion inside, just because that was the tradition. In the 'Star' and 'Castle' designs it was just possible to make this construction withstand the piston thrusts, with heavy bracing which makes access to the moving parts difficult in the extreme. In the 'King' it was not, and all the engines have been repaired, patched up and finally given new front ends. In other words, the engine is too powerful for its own strength.

There is, in total, little of the 1927 engine still extant. The boiler has been redesigned twice, with a larger superheater in 1947 and with a still larger superheater and double chimney in 1955. The bogie has been repeatedly modified from its beginning to the present day. Only last year,

January 1956, the entire class was abruptly grounded while the bogie frames were strengthened.

Of course, the 'Kings' have been made to work very well, saved by the quality of workmanship at Swindon Works and by the excellence of detail design. If the reader gets the chance to look at a Great Western engine stripped down, the elegance and simplicity of the components are a joy to behold. The difficulties of firing the long grate and servicing the inaccessible motion are regarded by the men as facts of life to which they must accustom themselves, and their opinions on the matter would not be sought anyway. From the commercial angle, those four big cylinders are ideal for lifting trains up the inclines in Devon, and at speed on the level they can do the work

on 18% cut-off, not drawing an undue amount of steam from what by current standards is a comparatively small boiler. In short, once you know of their inherent weaknesses, you realise what fine engines they are.

There are now 30 'Kings', but 31 were built; 20 in 1927, 10 in 1930 and one in February 1936, when No 6007 was damaged beyond repair in an accident and the new engine was given the same number and name. Starting with *King George V*, they were named after English kings in reverse order. In 1936 the last one, No 6029 *King Stephen*, was renamed *King Edward VIII*, and it is a measure of the popular support for that unhappy monarch that when the Government forced him to abdicate, the engine's name was retained and No 6028 *King Henry II* was renamed *King George VI*.

Left: **This is a 'King' which for some strange reason appeals to the writer; No 6029** *King Stephen*, **passing Acton on 9 May 1931. The train is a wonderful mixture: the first four are a 'Concertina' of 1906, a clerestory, a 'Dreadnought' and a 70ft 'Toplight'. The first and fifth coaches are in the crimson lake livery used from 1912 to 1922.** *E.R. Wethersett*

Below: **No 6029 carrying her later name of** *King Edward VIII*. *Ian Allan Library/LPC*

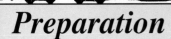

Preparation

In the MPD

On this fine summer morning, you cross Old Oak Common Lane, enter the gate on the corner and descend the long cinder path to the southwest corner of the shed. On your way to the office you pass a couple of the big '4700' class freight engines standing at rest after their night-time labours, and the spare engines, three 'Castles', fully prepared and ready to move out. Your first task is to sign on at the window of the time office, read the notices and find out what engine you have been allotted.

'Reading the Notices' is a vital part of your duty. In the time office are several huge notice boards with locked glass covers, in which are arrayed dozens of notices, sorted into those affecting all enginemen, those applying to certain jobs, temporary instructions, permanent orders, and so on. Important ones are out on desks and must be signed by the drivers.

The most important temporary notice this morning is that the up and down main lines are closed between Langley and Slough for engineering work. This is called a 'possession' and could cover anything from replacing a damaged rail to digging up and rebuilding the entire railway. For its duration, all traffic must use the relief lines, which constitute the northern pair of the four-track route. The notice goes on to state that trains are to be diverted to the Relief lines between West Drayton and Taplow, but

Below: **The interior of Old Oak Common engine shed in the early 1950s. Facing us across the turntable is a 'County' with the smokebox door open and alongside is BR Standard 4-6-2 No 70017** *Arrow*. **The other six engines round this table are all 'Halls'**. *A. E. Brown*

Above: **A standard Great Western cab. This one is a 'Hall', No 5900** *Hinderton Hall*. **Because the engine was unserviceable at the time, some parts are missing. The fine chain hanging from the roof is a whistle pull and should be hooked up on the left as it is on the right. The regulator is nearly full open and the brake handle above it is in the off position. The 'King' cab is slightly different in that the reverser screw is set further forward, giving the driver room to stand behind it.** *C. J. Austin*

that drivers should expect to be diverted at other points. The emphasis on this point is a recollection of the Norton Fitzwarren tragedy of 17 years ago: on a dark night, a driver forgot that he had been switched to the relief line, and only realised his mistake when a train on the main overtook him, too late to pull up before he reached a dead end.

On some routes, having to effect such a closure at short notice on a weekday morning would be an operational disaster. Here however, there will not be hordes of passengers fuming at the disruption. In its formative years the Great Western set out to attract wealthy patrons, not mass travel, and to this day there are no extra peak-time services to or from Paddington, except a couple of through trains from Windsor and Henley-on-Thames, whose arrival is timed to suit the boardroom rather than the shop floor. No express stops nearer than Reading. There is an hourly service for all stations to Slough, and another serving Southall, Hayes, West Drayton, Slough and all stations to Reading. The busiest period is not the early morning but between about 10 and 11 o'clock, and during this period there are scheduled freight train movements: Old Oak Common depot's coal train is booked to reach Hayes at about 9.45am and leave there at 10.18 to run through to the depot, arriving at

10.46; a trip goods from Paddington to Acton is on the relief line between Old Oak Common West and Acton from 10.40 to 10.45; a haul of empties leaves Southall at 10.12 bound for Severn Tunnel Junction; and there are others. All these freights can be shoved ruthlessly out of the way. A more serious problem is posed by the 9.42am Reading-Paddington, which runs up the relief line at a time when five expresses, including the 'Capitals United' and 'Cheltenham Spa', are coming up in close procession on the main. Clearly, even with the option of shunting the 'stopper' across to the main line platforms in Slough station, there are going to be delays, and the controllers at Paddington and Reading have to decide which trains are the more important. Those will be put through by a process known as 'forcing', which

Cab Controls, GWR 4-6-0 Engine

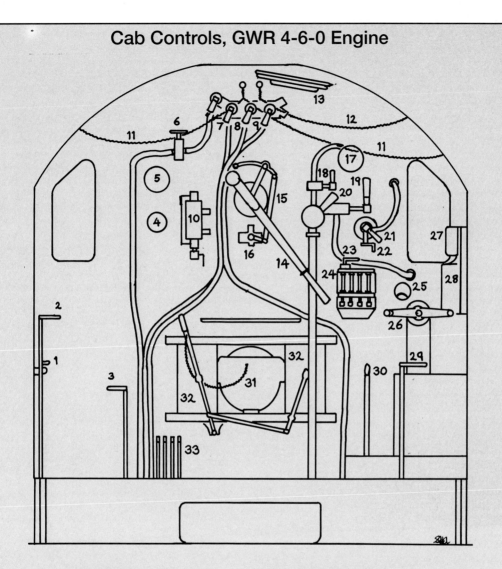

1	Hose-pipe tap	17	Vacuum gauge
2	Exhaust injector water regulator	18	Small ejector steam valve
3	Exhaust injector cone adjust	19	Large ejector steam valve
4	Train heat gauge	20	Brake application valve
5	Boiler pressure gauge	21	Blower
6	Train heat control valve	22	Lubricator warming cock
7	Exhaust injector live steam	23	Lubricator water cock
8	Exhaust injector supplementary steam	24	Hydrostatic lubricator
		25	Speedometer
9	Live injector steam	26	Reverser
10	Boiler water gauge	27	ATC bell
11	Whistle pull	28	ATC control box
12	Alarm whistle pull	29	Gravity sand handles
13	Lubricator condenser coil	30	Cylinder drain cocks
14	Regulator	31	Firedoor flap
15	Regulator jockey arm	32	Firedoors
16	Atomiser steam valve	33	Damper handles

Above: **A firebox flap in the down position, giving a view through the box to the tubes at the far end. The right-hand door is partially concealed by a cover intended to shield the driver's knees. This is a No 14 standard boiler on a 'Manor' class engine.** *C. J. Austin*

Above right: **A boiler pressure gauge, and beneath it a train heat pressure gauge. To the right is a handle operating the water gauge cocks. To the left is an open cab front window; a simple arrangement enabling the crew to clean the windows without leaving the cab.** *SHA*

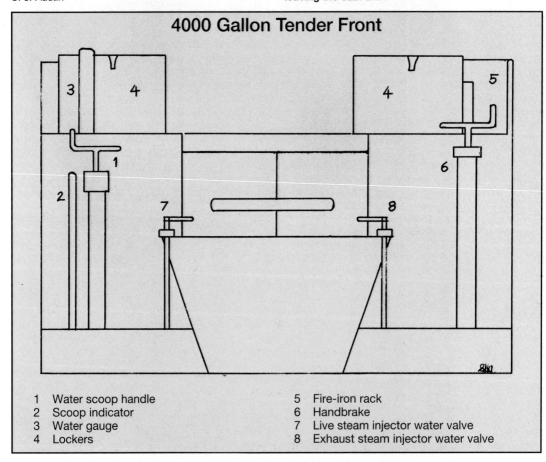

4000 Gallon Tender Front

1	Water scoop handle	5	Fire-iron rack
2	Scoop indicator	6	Handbrake
3	Water gauge	7	Live steam injector water valve
4	Lockers	8	Exhaust steam injector water valve

Table of Dimensions of Locomotives

	'King'	'Grange'	'1500'	'4500'
Overall length	68ft 2in	63ft 0in	33ft 0in	36ft 4in
Total weight	135^3/$_4$ tons	115^1/$_2$ tons	58 tons	57 tons
Firegrate area	34.3sq ft	27.07sq ft	17.4sq ft	16.6sq ft
Boiler diameter	6ft 0in	5ft 6in	5ft 0in	4ft 9in
Boiler tube length	16ft 5in	15ft 3in	10ft 8in	10ft 10in
Heating surface area	2,514sq ft	2,104sq ft	1,248sq ft	1,164sq ft
Boiler pressure	250psi	225psi	200psi	200psi
Cylinder bore	16^1/$_4$in	18^1/$_2$in	17^1/$_2$in	17in
Piston stroke	28in	30in	24in	24in
Coupled wheel dia	6ft 6in	5ft 8in	4ft 7^1/$_2$in	4ft 7^1/$_2$in
Coal capacity	6 tons	6 tons	3^1/$_2$ tons	3^3/$_4$ tons
Water capacity	4,000gal	4,000gal	1,350gal	1,000gal

means instructing the signalmen to pass them even if it means other trains being held back.

In the down direction it is not so bad. The 10.2am to Slough reaches there at 10.48 and if it is also shunted to the main platform, train No 130 will get past immediately afterwards. The 10.25am to Oxford is going to affect us on No 131, as we would normally overtake it while it makes a stop at Slough, and if it cannot be put out of our way, we will have to follow it until we regain the main line at Taplow. The next train down after us is a freight, the 10.35am Acton-Stoke Gifford, then there is about 15 minutes leeway before the 10.42am local to Reading and the 10.55 express to Pembroke Dock will be trying to get through the affected section at the same time.

The niceties of the operating problem are not in your mind as you stand looking at the notice. What occurs to you at once is that there is going to be a hold-up early in the run, the engine will be worked harder to make up the time, more coal will be burned than usual, and the one who will get to shift the extra coal is you.

In view of the altered crewing arrangements, the Running Foreman is looking out for you and greets you with a curt nod. You are pleased to find that you have been given engine No 6023 *King Edward II*, which is a good one. She has just returned from an intermediate overhaul at Swindon, but has not yet had a new front end fitted and is one of the last four 'Kings' retaining a single chimney at this time. You walk into the shed, where engines stand in their stalls; some sleeping silently, some hissing crossly at being woken up, some sighing and settling to their rest, some brooding aloof from the little figures who tend to their needs. Come on, they're only machines...

No 6023 is near the door in the 'bottom passenger' quarter, showing up clean in the misty gloom, the area around her largely clear, as other engines for the morning expresses have already gone out. On climbing up to the footplate, you see an overall jacket over the handbrake handle and a cloth tied to the reverser. This you recognise as a sign that your mate is already here and is underneath, examining and oiling the motion. When someone is squeezing themselves into the cramped space between the frames, not only a movement of the engine but someone moving the reverser and causing the radius rod of the valve motion to move could have fatal results. When you have stowed your bag in the driver's side tender toolbox, you get to work. Your first duty is to look at the boiler water gauge glass, in which the water level is showing halfway up. The engine is in steam, with a small fire heaped up on the back part of the grate and 100lb on the pressure gauge.

You take a handbrush and go forward, climb onto the front of the engine and open the smokebox door. The smokebox is empty of ash and there is no sign of leaks from any pipes or tube ends, so you clean round the door rim and its seating, close it and screw it up tight. Look round to see if there is any ash lying about on the front platform but the cleaners have done a good job and she is pretty smart. Check also that the sandboxes are full before returning to the cab.

Pull the fire-irons, dart, long and short prickers out of their rack on the fireman's side of the firebox, turn on the blower, open all the ashpan dampers, open the firehole doors and start pushing the fire forward, spreading it down the tunnel-like firebox. In the light of the flames which leap out of the opened fire you can look

down to the tubeplate and see whether any tube ends are blocked or leaking, and also check that the brick arch is intact. You will make the fire up gradually over the next half hour or so, allowing each new layer to ignite before adding more, aiming for an even thickness rising to a slight mound about 2ft in from the back. Besides the sliding doors the firehole has a flap plate, hinged at the bottom, which lies against the hole and has a chain to lift it. When up it leaves a gap at the top to admit some air over the fire, and in general you will use it from now on, leaving the doors open.

Behind you, looking likely to come down and bury you at any moment, is a mountain of coal piled way above the top of the tender and restrained by a quite inadequate pair of gates across the front between the two toolboxes. You drag down the biggest lumps with the coal pick and break them up to feed the fire. Long practice enables you to split them neatly into coconut size pieces. In between building the fire, you check that the required spanners, detonators, flags and spare gauge glasses are on board, the headlamps are filled and trimmed, and you have a tail lamp on the front buffer beam.

Your mate comes into the cab to replenish his oil feeder and collect a can of cylinder oil, which is warming over the firehole. He is, he says, looking forward to the diesels promised for next year or the year after. 'Then we'll be finished with this mucking about. Get in, press the starter and off you go. Easy as driving a car.'

You are not so sure. There won't be any job for a fireman on a diesel.

By the time your mate has done the outside oiling points and filled the mechanical lubricator on the front platform, boiler pressure has risen to 180lb and the two of you can test the injectors, the sanders and the vacuum brake ejector. Only if they are working perfectly is the engine fit to go. Satisfied, you can turn off the blower and shut the dampers. It is now time to take her outside to top up the tender. Nearly a ton of coal has gone into the firebox and on a long haul like the Plymouth job it is essential to leave the depot with as much coal as can be crammed onto the tender. The shed turntable man is aware of this and is looking out for you, so as soon as your mate gives him a shout, he brings the table round to your stall. Your mate is busy taking off his dirty overalls and waves

Left: **With tender stacked high and grey smoke rolling off the chimney, No 6028** *King George VI* **undergoes final preparation. This scene is just after the war, when standards of cleanliness have fallen. The locomotive in the ash road shelter on the left is No 4003** *Lode Star,* **destined to be preserved.** *Ian Allan Library*

Above: **On the disposal roads at Old Oak Common. This contraption is intended to receive ash shovelled out of the engine on the left and tip it into the wagon on the right. It is powered by vacuum from the engine's brake ejector, for which purpose a pipe is coupled up in the foreground. It is important to remember that the filthy task of disposing steam locomotives, which in the 1990s is a respectable hobby for elegant people, was in the 1950s the lowliest labouring job.** *LPC*

Centre right: **Waiting for the signal to move out from Old Oak Common yard, No 6004** *King George III* **on 6 June 1949.** *G. D. Brooks*

Right: **The '1500' class; a works photograph taken in August 1949. A product of the 'austerity' era, this machine is almost totally devoid of non-essential parts.** *British Railways*

towards the right-hand side of the cab, so you prepare to move her.

Incidentally, steam locomotives have this in common with ships, that they are frequently anthropomorphised by those who work with them, who, being men, use the feminine pronoun. There is no contradiction here. *King Edward II* is meant as a tribute to that gentleman, not a reincarnation of him.

The handbrake is jammed hard on, so you open the vacuum ejector again, then put the brake over to 'full on', so that the tender vacuum cylinder slams the blocks on even harder, freeing the handle so that you can spin it off. You wind the reverser into full forward, blow the whistle (which actually just gurgles), tug the regulator handle upwards just a little, and wait for something to happen. At the front end there is a spluttering from the cylinder drain pipes as first water, then spray, then steam, the breath of life to a railway engine, gushes out. As soon as you hear that happen you shut the regulator, looking down over the cab side for signs of movement. When she finally decides she is ready, the engine rolls forward quite quietly. You take hold of the brake handle again, listening to the wheels thump onto the table one by one, until on the last thump you put the brake on full and leave it on.

While the shed revolves very slowly round you, you are winding the reverser all the way to full back gear. Blow the whistle (which actually whistles this time) and after opening and shutting the regulator a couple of times more, she is off towards the doorway. Majestically the 'King' emerges into the morning sun, robed in green and crowned with gold, wreathed in gusts of steam, breathing heavily like a newly-awakened dragon. Your mate takes over to stop her at a water column while you scramble over the coal heap to reach the filler on the back of the tender. He then gets down to turn the water on, while you drop the pipe into the tank and see that it is filled bang up to the top. Then move on again, still backwards. These moves give you a chance to verify that the brakes are responding properly, that vacuum does not leak away when the ejector is shut off and the vacuum cylinders pivot freely in their trunnion mountings.

In order to take on some more coal, it will be necessary to interrupt the disposal men by going out to the points where engines are coming in, then run forward past the engines on the disposal roads, to back up to the west end of the coal stage and halt under the nearest 'tip'. On the floor of the stage, coalmen are filling little three-quarter-ton iron trolleys from loaded coal wagons. Above you one of them tips two trolleys of coal down and you trim it down with your shovel. Incidentally, shovelling coal on top of a heap, especially when you are standing on said heap, is quite the hardest part of the preparation, and you are happy to arrive back in the cab. Your mate is not there, for he has gone to make the tea, so you drive the engine away, retracing your route to the departure roads, finally to pull up right behind another 'King', the one for the 'Limited' proper, which is also just about ready to go off shed.

The old man who looks after the train numbers comes along and puts the '131' up on your smokebox. You start up your injector to replace the water used in moving, and while it is running use the hot water hose to damp the coal thoroughly and wash down the footplate. Since there are a few minutes to spare, you finish by wiping over the control handles, boiler backhead

Left: **No 1504 stabled in Old Oak Common engine shed. She has been on the empty carriage job, as she carries a battered target board numbered 11.**
B. E. Morrison

Above right: **Pannier tank No 1506 sets off up the ramp to the flyover with an empty train on 19 October 1963. Three up goods loops lie on the left, with the up relief line curving at the very edge of the picture. The overbridge carries Scrubs Lane.**
G. T. Robinson

and such of the fittings as are not too hot with a spare piece of cotton waste. Your mate appears with the last and most important pieces of equipment, the tea cans, and now you are ready.

With the Ups and Downs

While you are making your engine ready for the road, we are going to find the train. To do so is no minor expedition, for the Old Oak Common carriage depot is vast. It is built on what was once a common, part of the area we now call Wormwood Scrubs, bought by the railway in 1898. A shed covering 30 tracks, measuring 1,000ft long by 444ft wide, provides accommodation for 420 coaches. On its south side are 10 sidings called the 'Wall Side'. South of them is another group of 13 sidings called 'Field Sidings'. The 12 sidings between these and the main lines are the 'Up Yard' and are occupied by freight vehicles. On the north side of the shed are the 10 'Van Sidings', then the 'Coronation Sidings', 16 of them. At the far north of the site, close by the engine shed, is a carriage repair and paint shop, covering a further 10 tracks; this is the newest part of the depot, completed in 1939.

The grand total is 89 sidings, and that is not all. Because all these are dead-end roads, provision must be made for the engines of incoming trains to be released. Further out to the east are 21 reception roads for this purpose. At the far end are connections out to four running lines; up and down engine and carriage lines, which cross a flyover to the south side of the main lines, and up goods and down goods and carriage lines, which lie on the north side of the main lines. The flyover enables trains to leave the depot and run into the down, or departure, side of Paddington station without interfering with traffic on the main lines.

Empty trains leave Paddington on a down engine and carriage line, which joins the down goods line at Westbourne Park. The down line over the flyover only extends as far as Westbourne Park and is of little use except as an exit from the storage sidings of West London, Barlby Road and Portobello Depots. These complications are the result not of any master plan but of piecemeal enlargements taking place over more than a century.

If you look eastwards from Old Oak Common Lane, it is hard to realise that the whole of this area was once on a level with the road and has been dug away bit by bit as more sidings were laid down. There is always movement somewhere in this area, for there are five engines allocated to shunting in the yard, in addition to four in the freight sidings and up to 15 target

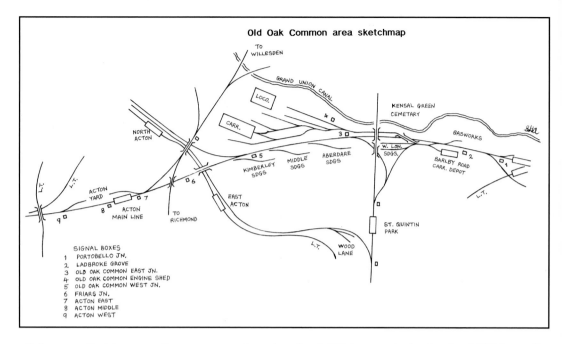

Old Oak Common area sketchmap

SIGNAL BOXES
1 PORTOBELLO JN.
2 LADBROKE GROVE
3 OLD OAK COMMON EAST JN.
4 OLD OAK COMMON ENGINE SHED
5 OLD OAK COMMON WEST JN.
6 FRIARS JN.
7 ACTON EAST
8 ACTON MIDDLE
9 ACTON WEST

pilots, so called because they carry numbered discs, working empty stock to and from Paddington.

The stock for train No 131, the 10.35am, is drawn up on one of the Coronation sidings ready to leave. It comprises 13 coaches. Last June two new sets of BR Standard coaches were provided for the 'Limited' and our train is similarly made up of smart new or refurbished stock. From the west end we have: a brake second; three open seconds; a GWR dining second; a GWR kitchen/dining first; two compartment firsts; two first/second composites; a brake second; a GWR composite slip coach; a composite.

The dining and kitchen coaches are from a batch built in 1932, which have always run as pairs. They were refurbished after the war by the firm of Hampton & Sons — one of the few occasions when the GWR bought any major equipment or services from outside. R. Woodfin in his *Cornwall Railway* centenary book said that the GWR produced 59 designs of kitchen car in the years 1896 to 1947, which displays exemplary energy in the drawing office if nothing else. The slip coach was built in 1938 and has run in the 'Cornish Riviera' or its equivalent ever since. The other coaches were all new last year. The whole ensemble is painted in a brown and pale yellow livery, sometimes said to be Great Western.

The train seats 376 second class passengers and 156 first class; it is 830ft long and weighs, unloaded, 420 tons. With a full load of holidaymakers and luggage it will probably weigh about 460 tons, reducing to about 390 tons after the slip portion is detached. This is comfortably within the load limit for a 'King' of 500 tons from Paddington to Newton Abbot and 485 tons from Wellington to Whiteball, but is over the limit of 360 tons from Newton Abbot to Brent. (Between the wars 'Kings' regularly took 16-coach trains weighing nearly 600 tons.)

At the east end we find a real ugly duckling of a locomotive. It looks as though a respectable Great Western tank engine has had a shameful liaison with a US 'switcher', and that is in some sort what happened. The US engines bought by the Southern Railway for shunting at Southampton Docks were shipped into Newport Docks, and Swindon was so impressed by their mechanical layout that it produced its own version, with a taper boiler and pannier tanks; the '1500' class. They were designed for shunting in marshalling yards, a function which in 1949 was rapidly being turned over to diesel locomotives, so only 10 were built. With their short wheelbase and outside cylinders they are wildly unsteady at anything like speed, so they are quite useless for the general range of pannier tank duties. At present there are one each at Southall, Didcot and Cardiff, three in Newport, and four at Old Oak Common, which the management with typical British flair have put to a job for which they were not intended: working empty trains in and out of Paddington. This example is No 1504. She is standing quietly with no smoke visible; her fireman made up his fire in the deep square box some while ago and will not touch it until this run is over.

Right: **Seen from Westbourne Park platform, on 8 May 1962, this empty train is going round the back of Portobello Junction box. Engine No 1504 is passing one of the automatic signals which control the carriage lines.** *IA Library*

Below: **East of Westbourne Park on 23 November 1963. No 9659 is working up the engine and carriage line past Subway Junction box. To the left of the box the LT electric lines go down into their underpass. Further left is the Crimea Yard. The main lines are immediately to the right of the train. The wagons partly obscured by the steam are in Paddington New Depot.** *G. T. Robinson*

Just after 9.30am we are called forward by the shunter and see the signal being lowered for us to leave the yard. Train No 130 has only just left and is actually in sight up ahead, but the engine and carriage lines are operated on a Permissive Block system, allowing trains to be brought up nose to tail if necessary. They are controlled by three-aspect colour light signals, each with a calling-on light which allows you to pass the red

and approach the train in front. The way ahead lies up the 1 in 39 gradient onto the flyover, but that is no problem for No 1504. Our driver puts her into full forward gear and opens the regulator slightly, whereon she shoulders forward without much effort. He opens out gradually to full regulator and the exhaust beat booms deafeningly from the firehole, accompanied by rhythmic flashes of light which anticipate a

Left: **A view of Paddington's approaches from above Platform A, taken in August 1967, shortly before the whole lot was ripped out. The water tank at the bottom is beside the siding used by empty stock pilots waiting for their return loads. At the top is Bishops Road bridge, with Paddington Arrival box in front of it. The top left area is occupied by the goods station, with the Grand Union Canal out of sight behind it. The four furthest platforms are electrified for the use of LT trains.** *British Railways*

Right: **The writer generally manages to work in a picture of a certain locomotive, and here she is, by courtesy of the Merchant Navy Locomotive Preservation Society, in Paddington Platform 1 on 22 September 1994. The important item in this photograph is the GWR War Memorial, visible ahead of the engine. Brunel's roof and Wyatt's decoration are kept in first class order but the three-faced clock no longer works.** *R. L. Sewell*

dance-hall craze by a generation, as she drags the load slowly but surely up the incline.

From the top we can see down to Westbourne Park station and the grey mass of London, contrasting with the green of Kensal Green Cemetery just below us. On the way down our speed tops the 15mph limit and the driver puts the brake on to steady her when the rock 'n' roll action gets a bit uncomfortable. On the level he gives her more steam and the engine waddles steadily along. On the right-hand side of the spread of tracks, we go round the back of Westbourne Park station, close to the LT line where a red Underground train comes round its curve and gallops ahead, down into the underpass which takes it over to between the main and goods lines.

Ahead a signal gives us a red as an engine is crossed over to Ranelagh Bridge servicing point, but it clears almost at once and we roll on into the canyon between Paddington Goods on the left and the parcels station on the right. Here again is a red signal and we creep up to it, only just moving. When it changes, the engine is opened out to drag the coaches over the array of crossings, round the sharp curve into Paddington station. Train 130 is in Platform 2 and we are put into Platform 3. The clank of No 1504's motion and the air pump's spits resound from the high roof as she approaches the dead

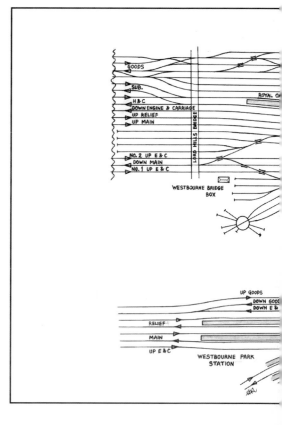

end, slower and slower until the last brake application brings her to a halt almost touching the buffer stops. Her fireman uncouples, fills his boiler, closes his firedoor and dampers, and then busies himself doing nothing for half an hour.

Paddington station was designed by I.K. Brunel in 1854. It lies in the valley of the Westbourne, which is why it is aligned towards the nearby Serpentine in Hyde Park and has that inconvenient curve at the north end. Its immediate ancestors are the Palm House in Kew Gardens and the glasshouses at Chatsworth House, both of which may still be seen for comparison. The cross-arches clearly derive from the former, and in this case served to make room for the turntables and cross-connecting tracks which were usual in stations in those days. There was no attempt to house the offices in impressive architecture; the range of buildings alongside Platform 1 are undistinguished and have no exterior, for the platforms are below the outside street level. From the stops, No 1504 is looking across an extension dating from 1933, the covered area called 'The Lawn', towards the Great Western Hotel and Underground station entrances. At the other end, the platforms outside the main roof are also 1933 extensions,

and on the east side the gloomy area beyond the cab road is an addition of 1909. Across Platform 1 are the unique Post Office, the suite of rooms provided for royalty, and further down, a bay window marking the Great Western boardroom, with the War Memorial beneath it.

Meanwhile, back on No 6023...

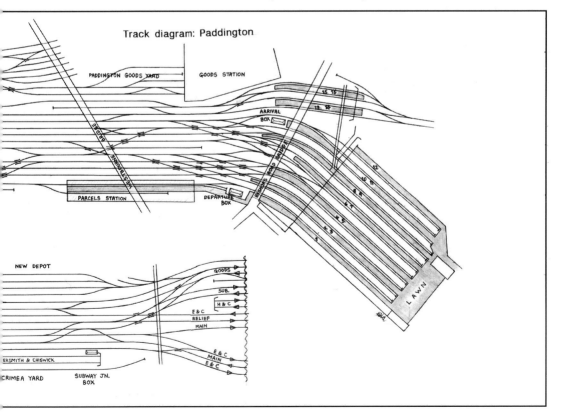

Track diagram: Paddington

PADDINGTON GOODS YARD   GOODS STATION

ARRIVAL BOX

PARCELS STATION

DEPARTURE BOX

NEW DEPOT

GOODS
SUB.
H & C
E & C
RELIEF
MAIN

ERSMITH & CHISWICK

CRIMEA YARD   SUBWAY JN. BOX

E & C
MAIN
E & C

LAWN

Schedule: Cornish Riviera

MON-FRI

m.ch	Train No	130 Special Load	131***
0.00	Paddington dep	10.30am ML	10.35am ML
1.17	Westbourne Park	10.34	10.39
9.03	Southall	10.42$\frac{1}{2}$	10.48
18.33	Slough	10.50$\frac{1}{2}$	10.56$\frac{1}{2}$
24.16	Maidenhead	10.55$\frac{1}{2}$	11.2
30.78	Twyford	11.1$\frac{1}{2}$	11.8
35.75	Reading	11.6	11.13
53.04	Newbury	11.23$\frac{1}{2}$	11.33
66.30	Bedwyn	11.38$\frac{1}{2}$	11.48
70.05	Savernake LL	11.43	11.52$\frac{1}{2}$
81.04	Patney	11.53	12.2$\frac{1}{2}$pm
94.42	Heywood Road Jn	12.3pm	12.15
96.64	Fairwood Jn	12.5	12.17
100.04	Clink Road Jn	12.8	12.20
102.22	Blatchbridge Jn	12.10	12.22
115.21	Castle Cary	12.24 ML	12.36
142.55	Taunton	12.46 ML	1.3
153.44	Whiteball Tunnel	12.56$\frac{1}{2}$	1.16
172.17	Cowley Bridge Jn	1.12$\frac{1}{2}$	1.33
173.36	Exeter St David's	1.14$\frac{1}{2}$	1.35
184.01	Dawlish Warren	1.27	1.47
193.51	Newton Abbot arr	1.40	2.1
	dep	1.43 AE	2.4 AE
194.59	Aller Jn	1.45	2.6$\frac{1}{2}$
197.44	Dainton Siding	1.49	2.12
202.29	Totnes	1.56	2.20
206.58	Rattery	2.4$\frac{1}{2}$	2.30
209.18	Brent	2.7	2.33
218.65	Hemerdon	2.20	2.44
223.74	Lipson Jn	2.26	2.50
225.40	Plymouth NR arr	2.30	2.55
	dep	2.38	3.3
226.05	Devonport Jn	2.40	3.5
229.15	Royal Albert Bridge	2.45	3.10
229.57	Saltash	2.47	3.12
243.22	Liskeard	3.6	3.32
252.33	Bodmin Road	3.19	3.45
260.17	Par arr	3.30	3.56
	dep	3.33	4.0
279.14	Truro arr	4.3	4.29
	dep	4.8	4.33
279.67	Penwithers Jn	4.10	4.35
284.31	Chacewater	4.17	4.42
291.69	Camborne	4.28	4.53
294.30	Gwinear Road arr	4.32	4.57
	dep	4.34	5.0
299.29	St Erth arr	4.41	5.10
	dep	4.44	5.13
305.01	Penzance arr	4.55	5.23

Notes: 130: Westbury slip arr 12.13pm, conveyed in 11.45am Chippenham-Weymouth.
Slip coach conveyed in train 131 when running.
Assisting engine to go through Newton Abbot-Plymouth if taken.

131 Runs if required.
Conveys Westbury slip
coach when runs.

The Royal Road

At 10 o'clock you are away from the shed. The first event as you leave the yard is a loud squawk from a box beside the driver. A moment later the brakes come on and, if the driver did not lift a small handle on the box, would stop her. This is a most important item, and you should take a moment to think about it.

The Great Western brake is superior to any other vacuum system, the result of a comprehensive development effort led by Joseph Armstrong at the turn of the century. It uses a vacuum level of 25 inches of mercury, instead of the 21in adopted by all other railways. To produce this the engines have not only a very effective steam-operated ejector but also a mechanical pump whose valves make the characteristic spitting sound while the engine is moving. At more than about 15mph the pump can maintain vacuum, which saves steam and makes the engine a little quieter in motion. A small-jet ejector is provided to supplement it if necessary. An important invention was the direct admission valve, which responds to a rise in train pipe pressure by admitting air from the atmosphere, thus achieving a quicker application than would be obtained if all the air had to come down the pipe from the driver's brake valve. These two

Below: **No 6026 *King John* preparing to leave Paddington Platform 3. She has a full head of steam and steam is issuing from the chimney as her driver blows the brake off. This view is undated but must be near the end of the engine's life, judging from the leaks from glands, anti-vacuum valves and even the whistle.** *Ian Allan Library*

features give more and faster stopping power. Quick response is also the reason why the larger passenger engines have vacuum brakes, although others have steam brakes linked to the vacuum system.

And of course there is Automatic Train Control (ATC). A metal ramp at each distant signal lifts a shoe on the engine, breaking an electric circuit which holds shut a cock in the train pipe. The cock opens, applies the brake and sounds an air horn. If the signal is at clear, an electric current is passed through the ramp, through the shoe, operates switches to keep the brake cock closed and ring a bell in the cab, and returns to earth through the wheels. This was the first really dependable system of cab-signalling and the GW men still think it is the best. When, after the war, the Government announced its intention to adopt the 'four-aspect' signal system, the GW engineers argued that the two levels of caution signal it gives should have distinctive cab signals. They redesigned the ATC to provide this and staged a spectacular demonstration on 12 October 1947, in which a train was driven at almost 100mph up to a yellow signal. The driver stood back, leaving the engine going full out, and the ATC brought it to a dead stop inside the red.

To return to the present, you have just been over an ATC test ramp at the shed exit. During

Left: **The relay box and bell, mounted against the cab side window. On this side of the box is a handle which the driver lifts to regain control of the brake after a caution signal.** *SHA*

Below left: **Viewed from Platform A, No 6013** *King Henry VIII* **with the 1.30pm to Plymouth, under Westbourne Bridge. The train is in GWR livery although the date is 7 May 1948. The engine is passing over an ATC ramp and the bell will ring in a moment, the contact shoe being under the cab.** *C. C. B. Herbert*

Above right: **Train No 131, the 10.35am Paddington-Penzance, passing West London Depot repair shops on 4 April 1958, hauled by 'Castle' No 4090** *Dorchester Castle.* **Almost concealed by the silhouette of the engine's lubricator pump is the tail of a train on the flyover. Kensal Green Cemetery lies behind the wall.** *M. H. C. Baker*

Right: **'Britannias' worked down to Penzance in the early 1950s; this is Cardiff-based No 70027** *Rising Star* **on the 3.45pm to Fishguard, with West Ealing station in the background. Above the engine the Greenford loop diverges from the relief lines. Beyond are West Ealing box and the milk depot with two tank wagons. On the far side is a prewar Austin estate car parked in Manor Road.** *R. E. Vincent*

the run up, on the same engine and carriage line as the empty stock, which is taken under easy steam to avoid livening up the fire, you have to decide whether you have enough in the box. Eventually you compromise by lobbing a few more lumps down each side. You now have 210lb on the gauge.

Backing slowly up to the train, you open the firedoor and raise the flap, and turn the blower on a touch to avoid any show of smoke. Your mate stops her for you to get off and signal him back; although that is not really necessary, as even though he is on the blind side of the curve, he brakes so that she just compresses the buffers and, with the brake hard on, does not bounce back. You duck under the buffers, lift the vacuum hoses off their stoppers, drop your screw coupling over the coach drawhook and tighten it up, then couple the vacuum hoses. When you return to the cab your mate is out on the platform

giving his name to the guard. The latter has already walked the length of the train twice, to examine it outside and in, and will now walk back to the rear to collaborate in testing the brake. Create vacuum, check that at least 21in shows on the gauge in the rear coach, check that it does not fall when the ejector is shut off. Make a full application and check that the train pipe vacuum does not rise by leakage from the reservoir chambers, then make another test application from the guard's brake valve. You will appreciate the importance of these tests when the train includes a slip coach with an automatic sealing valve in its train pipe connector. The time is now 10.25.

The brake tests, important as they are, are not directly your concern. You take the headlamps up to place them on the front; then you can have a well-earned cup of tea, wash down the floor again, and put a little water in to hold pressure just below 250lb. Dampers can be opened again; you have an impressive array of them on a 'King', as the ashpan is in two parts, ahead and astern of the rear coupled axle, with two dampers for each, so you choose the two front ones.

At 10.30 whistles blow up and down the platform, there is a roar of steam from the 'King' ahead and to your left, and 130 starts to move. That has the effect of sending your passengers scurrying for the doors, so four minutes later when your starter signal turns green, the platform is almost empty and the Platform Inspector can see clearly down to the green flag held up by the slip guard. You are both leaning out of the left side of your cab. The Inspector shows you his green flag. Your mate crosses to his side, pulls the whistle chain, winds his reverser into full forward and opens the regulator slightly.

Steam roars out of the front, filling the space between the platforms. The engine gives a heave. Another, and again, and again. He shuts the cylinder cocks and you become aware of the deep bark from the chimney. Your mate suddenly snaps the regulator shut and immediately afterwards there are several rapid barks while the engine bounces. He opens up again and she gets a grip. Over the crossings, finding the straight, seeing his green signals, he eases the regulator handle up a little more. You are not watching this; you are looking back at the train emerging from the station roof until you are satisfied that it is all there. You give a wave to some men on Platform A who are watching, and turn to look at your pressure gauge — 240lb.

The engine is nosing from side to side and rolling from the piston thrusts, but abreast of Royal Oak platform your mate starts winding his reverser back, she steadies up and the exhaust quietens. The ATC bell rings out cheerfully at each green signal — Subway Junction, Portobello Junction, Ladbroke Junction. Over to the right, a pannier tank is on the up Sub line with a van train; that is the Acton to Smithfield freight, which is due to stand at Royal Oak until 10.50, before it ventures into the Metropolitan Line tunnel beneath the streets of the city. A swish and a clatter close by; the 7.55am 'Cheltenham Spa Express', dashing for the terminus. Another follows very closely; the 3.55am boat train from Fishguard Harbour. Our home shed lies far away to the right as our 'King' heads down between the yards. The regulator is now wide open, reverser back to 20% cut-off and she is riding smoothly and quietly. You turn on the exhaust steam injector, pick up the shovel and turn to address the coal.

The grate is just over 10ft long, level for the rear third then sloping down to the front. Firing it is not just a matter of throwing coal 10 feet. If you lift a shovelful off the tender shovelling plate and swing it through the firehole, it will either hit the deflector plate just inside, or clear that and strike the end of the brick arch, and not reach the front. No, you must lift the shovel and swing it downwards to the firehole, using the rim as a fulcrum to bounce the coal over the back of the fire. Naturally, you put as much as you dare on the back, so that the slope and the pull of the blast help to roll it down forwards. Eight shovels form a round, after which you flick the flap up, glance at the gauge glass and look ahead to spot the next signal. The effort of the start has consumed a lot of water but it has also whipped the fire into blazing white and you have to open the injector water tap a little more to keep her from blowing off.

We are now passing through Acton Main Line station at 50mph and you step across to see if there is anything interesting in the yard. As the main marshalling point for the London area it is always busy, with five shunting engines at work. Just now we might see a Midland engine which has come in from Brent yard, or an Eastern Region 'J50' tank dropping down the ramp from Acton Wells with the 9.35am from Temple Mills. (Sometimes one might catch two more of these transfer trip workings on the West London line where it crosses above Old Oak Common: the 10.0am Willesden to Shepherds Bush and the 10.15am Lillie Bridge to Willesden are booked to pass North Pole Junction at half past ten.)

Speed tops 60mph as we approach Ealing Broadway, linked up further to about 17% so the exhaust is no more than a bass background to

Above right: **A view west from Southall station, over the marshalling yard where two engines shunt continuously, at about 11.30am on 12 April 1952. The train is the 4.55am from Fishguard, hauled by 'Castle' No 5002** *Ludlow Castle.* **Beyond the engine is a yard used by the Cambrian Wagon Works, and behind that the warehouse of LeGrand Sutcliff & Gell Ltd. The 1933 colour-light signalling comes to an end here, and the signals visible are colour-lights on the running lines and semaphores for the sidings.** *J. C. Flemons*

Right: **The oil warning gauge on a 'King'.** *SHA*

Far right: **Showing the regulator handle just open in what is called 'drifting steam' position. The upward projecting arm raises the curved slotted link, opening a steam supply which blows oil into the cylinders. At the bottom the firebox flap is raised, with the doors partly closed over it.** *C. J. Austin*

Right: **On a Sunday in 1960, a train of milk tanks returning empty to South Wales passes Southall engine shed. The engine is the preserved No 6024** *King Edward I*, **in final form with a double chimney. On the right is a BR diesel railcar, used on the Uxbridge and Staines branches; outside the shed is one of the five diesel parcels railcars, and beside the shed in the distance is one of the GWR railcars.** *M. Pope*

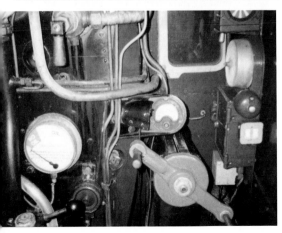

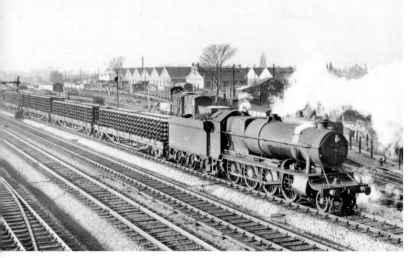

Left: **A train load of 60ft track lengths standing on the down relief line, west of West Ealing station, on 28 November 1959. The engine, 2-8-0 No 4706, has been commandeered for the day in between her normal duties of hauling night express goods trains. She has a leak, visible on the boiler side, in a pipe carrying oil to the regulator valve. Beyond, a pannier tank is shunting in the Permanent Way Dept sidings.**
K. L. Cook

the ticking of the air pump. Through some more bridges and we are running on the Wharncliffe Viaduct over the Brent Valley, with views of a golf course on the right and Osterley Park to the left. From here for the next 12 miles is a continuous succession of yards and rail-served factories, ironically a consequence of the GWR's early passenger policy. An undeveloped corridor was left on this side of London. Much of the land was still green in the 1920s, when the company decided it was time to drum up some business. An advertising campaign was backed up by free excursions for potential factory builders, inviting them to 'Come and see the sites'. This policy was further boosted by the evacuation of bombed-out London factories during World War 2, and a number of famous commercial names now reside along here: the London Co-op; Daimler; AEC; Scott & Browne; Quaker Oats; Tickler's Jam; Batchelor's Peas; Electrical & Musical Industries; the Gramophone Company ('His Master's Voice'); McAlpine; ICI; McMichael Radio; Horlicks. West of Slough the Slough Trading Estate has its own siding system, and by the line at Reading is Huntley & Palmer's biscuit factory. Southall locomotive depot provides men and machines for shunting all these sidings and for long-distance freight hauls.

As we race through the station, a transfer trip from Acton is standing in the back road after its 10.35 arrival, and one of the unlovely ex-Ministry of Supply 2-8-0s is waiting at the platform end for us to clear before it departs to run light to Banbury. Immediately afterwards we overtake a freight on the down relief line, the 10.35am Acton to Stoke Gifford, its '2800' class engine ambling along with casual ease.

Here you turn the injector off, having a mind to the diversion coming up. Passing Hayes box, your mate opens the blower a little and shuts the regulator down to drifting steam. A couple of

minutes later the West Drayton East distant comes into sight, on as expected, and he starts braking down to the 25mph required to negotiate the main to relief line crossover; the squawk from the ATC as we pass the signal he silences at once. The signalman is clearly taking no chances and only lowers his home when we are coming slowly up to it. The engine turns abruptly right and left, and carries on through the platforms, now with the characteristic high-pitched puffs of a Swindon product running under easy steam.

As soon as he has transferred train No 131 from main to relief, the West Drayton East signalman telephones West Drayton West to tell him just that, and both men note the call in their train registers. The message is sent on from box to box until the train is returned to its normal line.

The reference to 'drifting steam' could do with a little explanation. Valves and pistons are lubricated by an oil mist blown in by a jet of steam, and that steam is turned on by the initial travel of the regulator handle. The high steam temperature delivered by the modern superheated boilers is treated with great respect, and the driver has a large, fierce-looking gauge in front of him. It is a pressure gauge, but shows only a red sector labelled 'NO OIL' and a white sector labelled 'OIL'. A legend below these reads 'When running with steam shut off move regulator from full shut position until pointer shows in white sector'. Another reason for not shutting off completely is that the exhaust steam injector draws steam from the blast pipe. If there is no exhaust it stops, and you have to turn on its live steam supply and adjust its movable combining cone to get it working again.

While your mate is accelerating to the 60mph limit, you are watching ahead with enhanced attention, for where there are men working on the track there is a possibility of one of them

Above: **Please forgive the diesel locomotive in this view of the west end of Slough station, showing that in 1963 it retained some of the ornate features befitting its former royal status. The train, a Class D partly-fitted freight, is on the down relief line. At that time the Ford Motor Co was sending out trainloads of vehicles from Slough.** *P. J. Lynch*

wandering into your path. A group of wagons loaded with track panels appears near Langley station, followed by other vehicles, sleeper wagons, ballast hoppers, tool vans, two cranes and squads of men. On a bright day such as this the latter are easy to spot even in their dark overalls, but in darkness it is a different matter and a steam engine is a very quiet beast when it is coming towards you.

At this point we get signals on again, so you turn on the live steam injector and ladle a good covering of coal over the rear of your fire to cool it temporarily. Sure enough Dolphin Junction stops us, but just as you are about to get down to go to the box, he lowers his home signal. The halt alerts passengers to their surroundings, quite a good place to do so as they can see over the town and the Thames meadows to the tower of Windsor Castle. Getting under way again, you see that Slough East is also just lowering his home, so

clearly the 10.25am Oxford has made its stop and is pulling away just ahead. It was due to leave here at 11.1, whereas we would have passed at 10.56½. Just beyond the station, standing on the main line is a rake of coaches which can only be the Windsor branch train, also delayed by the engineering work. Our slow passage of the station enables us to notice the unusually elaborate decoration of the place. The first royal train journeys were made over this line, and should there be a pause in the royal progress onto the Windsor branch, it was essential that anything visible from the royal window was suitable for the royal eye.

At Taplow your mate slows down, the relief to main signal is off as expected, and we are back on track. You look back to watch the train undulating over the crossover. It has gone remarkably smoothly, we are only eight minutes behind schedule, you have a full boiler and full steam. The road stretches ahead straight and level. Here you are on an embankment, with on both sides the well-wooded Thames Valley, glorious on this fine morning after stifling London. From the footplate Maidenhead Bridge appears merely as a low wall on either side. Here is the Oxford train on the relief line, stopping at Maidenhead station as we hurtle through. As we thought, there is a traffic jam on the up lines, and

Left: **Spring in the Thames Valley, but late in the day for steam. 0-6-0 No 2248 has lost her numberplates. The Henley branch freight comes into Twyford on 22 April 1964.** *B. K. Snow*

Right: **The down 'Limited' at East Park Farm, a mile west of Twyford. No 6020** *King Henry IV* **is purring along, with just a trace of grey smoke from the chimney.** *R. F. Dearden*

Below right: **Sonning Cutting, with 'County' No 1002** *County of Berks* **on the 11.15am to Worcester, under the Bath Road bridge. This shows how, when the line was widened in 1890, the cutting sides were cut back and retaining walls were built to obtain more space. The original broad gauge tracks lay in the middle arch.** *M. Pope*

Maidenhead West, Waltham and Shottesbrook all have trains standing at their signals.

The 'King' is going well now and keeping you pretty busy — flap down, eight shovels, flap up, check feed, break lumps, damp down. Welsh coal tends to be dusty; now that she is hot you can fire some dust with the lumps, but keep it well watered. Take a breather, and you can exchange greetings with a friend on a pannier tank standing in Ruscombe siding with a freight, the 10.7am Slough to Reading West. He should have left Ruscombe at eleven.

The railway cuts straight across the meanders of the river, through slightly higher ground. Before rejoining the Thames at Reading it passes through Sonning Hill in a great cutting which is one of the biggest engineering works on the line. Under a high bridge carrying the Bath Road, the massive gasholders of Reading Gasworks come into sight.

Reading likes to see itself described in terms like 'modern' and 'bustling', although it is a market town of some antiquity. As we come alongside the river, we cross over a waterway, the mouth of the River Kennet. This was made navigable in 1723 and later became part of a London to Bristol water route in conjunction with the River Avon and the Kennet & Avon Canal. The construction of the railway along the same route was much assisted by this highway but of course once in operation it killed the canal. Bought up by the Great Western and now the property of British Transport Waterways, who are legally required to make a show of keeping it open, the canal is seen from the train in the form

of odd stretches of water, buildings and locks presenting scenes of picturesque decay.

Now we pass through Reading station, which was the last of Brunel's 'one-sided' stations to be replaced by a conventional layout in 1897. Below us to the right is the Signal Works. Not only signals, but level crossing installations, telegraph instruments, ATC equipment, complete locking frames and even partially prefabricated signal boxes are turned out here. It is typical of a company that never used anyone else's product if they could design and make their own. Speaking of signalling, the popular expert Adrian Vaughan has pointed out the paradox that train No 130, the premier express on the GWR, is telegraphed through Reading as a branch passenger train, because it turns left at Reading Main Line West onto what is at that point the branch. A speed limit of 40mph applies to this turn; on this occasion, instead of drifting down to that speed your mate brakes quite sharply, determined to make up time where possible. Thanks to the excellence of GWR switched diamonds, the engine takes the junction easily, just swaying a little. Your mate looks across to you and asks if you are willing and able to give him the extra steam he wants to make up the delay. What he actually says is:

'You all right to go?'

Your reply is equally succinct: 'OK.' Conversation on the footplate is kept to the absolute minimum while running, if only because the noise makes talking very difficult. You leave the fire alone for a minute while he whips her up, the noise of *KE* working in 30%

708

cut-off bringing the Oxford Road signalman to his window. There is a down grade past Southcote, the last respite for you before a 30-mile climb of gradually increasing gradient to Savernake. When he has linked her up again you resume shovel and flap work. This goes on for another 10 minutes, until it is time to make the first water pick-up from Aldermaston trough. As the little station whirls by you unhook a chain from the right-hand handle on the tender front and wind the handle a little. You do not really need the marker board with its zigzag line to show you the trough, and you wind the scoop down until you feel a jar as it hits the water. Spray erupts under the tender and from the two vents on top. At this speed, a good 70, the drag on the scoop holds it down and you feel a momentary panic that you will not be able to get it out before the tender overflows. The vents spurt water, then by sheer luck the up gradient at the end of the trough lifts the scoop clear, leaving you relieved, if rather wet. You wind it up and put the chain back on. The tangible radiance from the fire will soon dry you off.

The Berks & Hants line is more rural in character than the old main line and has several level crossings. The first is at Ufton, a mile east of Aldermaston, and there are eight more on the way to Taunton. At each crossing is a similar scene: a lane off the Bath Road, the railway, a signal box, a canal bridge, a lock house and perhaps a couple more cottages; the whole a serene picture, brought briefly to life as a train thunders by. There are not all that many trains; we pass just two, the 7.15am Plymouth to Paddington express and the 9.27am Westbury to Reading local, before reaching Newbury. All this time you are managing to keep your pressure up around 240lb, with the feed on all the time, the regulator wide open and the reverser on 20%.

Here is Thatcham West, 50 miles in one hour from Paddington, not bad considering the diversion. All boards are off through Newbury, so 130 must be doing equally well and keeping clear ahead. Newbury is a typical market town made prosperous by being in the middle of a horse-breeding district. An oddity is that the firm of Plenty & Co at Newbury Wharf built the first RNLI lifeboats. On our right the Didcot, Newbury & Southampton line curves in under a road bridge and on it we glimpse a '2251' class engine with three coaches, the 10.50am Didcot to Eastleigh which Newbury East has held for us. Your mate reaches up to pull the whistle chain. This is the only move he has made in the last quarter of an hour, and you wonder if it would be possible for a driver to fall asleep on a nonstop

Left: **A down express runs out of Sonning Cutting, past Sonning signalbox. The engine is 'Star' No 4034** *Queen Adelaide.* **The photograph is undated but the grey carriage roofs place it in the postwar period.** *Real Photographs*

Right: **The view from Reading Main Line West signalbox, where the Berks & Hants Line branches left and the main line goes straight on. Between the two lies the locomotive depot, with the repair shop prominent. In the distance a BR Class 9 2-10-0 is on a train in the up yard. On the right is Reading Goods Lines West signalbox, and below it a pannier tank is working with its shunters' truck coupled behind.** *C. J. Blay*

run, and if anyone would notice. You watch through the station, verify all the signals and resume flap and shovel work.

Coincidentally, you see another DNS train waiting at Enborne Junction, a northbound one also stopped for us. The engine on this one makes you look twice, for there is something funny about its frames and wheels; it is *City of Truro.* After 25 years in York Museum she was overhauled at Swindon during February this year, and besides being on offer for special trains is used on ordinary workings. She is in fact the first preserved standard gauge locomotive to be restored to main line running order. What possessed British Railways to enter the

preservation game and how the expenditure was sneaked through the system is another story which may one day be told.

Your mate moves again to snick the reverser over a notch. He does that twice more in the next 10 minutes, until by the time you get to Bedwyn the exhaust is coming out in a full-bodied roar. He has averaged a mile a minute from Reading, picking up five minutes on schedule, and don't you know it. The fire is thinner than you would like, but that is the way to keep her really hot, as long as you are able to keep feeding it without pause. If anything goes wrong, such as a hole in it, you will know right away as the pressure will drop in short order.

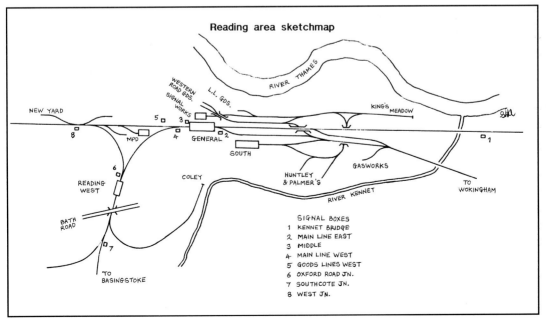

Reading area sketchmap

SIGNAL BOXES
1 KENNET BRIDGE
2 MAIN LINE EAST
3 MIDDLE
4 MAIN LINE WEST
5 GOODS LINES WEST
6 OXFORD ROAD JN.
7 SOUTHCOTE JN.
8 WEST JN.

Above left: **The important feature in this photograph of an up Plymouth express entering Reading is the signal, which is Main Line West's up home. The two distant arms low down are for use when a slip coach is to be detached. They indicate whether the train has a clear road past Main Line East and will not be stopped in the station, so it is safe for the slip coach guard to cast off. In this case the train is clear to the up main.** M. W. Earley

Left: **This is such an excellent view of a 'King' picking up water at speed that we hope readers will not mind that it is not on the Plymouth route, but is at Aynho troughs on the Birmingham line.**
A. A. Vickers

Above: **Something away to the right has caught the attention of the fireman on No 6029** King Edward VIII **as he starts from Newbury on the 11.30am Paddington-Plymouth in August 1961. This was then the last 'King' job on the West of England line. The 2.45am Tavistock Jn-Acton freight is passing on the up through road.** B. H. Kimber

Being so occupied you have no eyes for the scenery, the canal lying a few yards from the line all the way. The Kennet Navigation terminates at Newbury Wharf and this is the artificial cut, constructed between 1794 and 1810. It rises through 30 locks to a summit level extending from Crofton to Wootton Rivers, corresponding of course to the railway summit at Savernake, but suffering from the need to supply water to the topmost section. On our left just before Wolfhall Junction (named after King Wulfhere who lost a

battle here) is a reservoir, Wilton Water, and on our right an engine house with a prominent chimney. It contains two steam pumping engines, an 1836 Sims and an 1812 Boulton & Watt, which are the oldest working steam plant in the world. They lift water into a leat which feeds the summit level at the point where canal and main line go under the Midland & South Western Junction Railway. The canal passes beneath Savernake Low Level station in a tunnel, emerging on the north side of the railway.

If you look to the left now, you will see another 0-6-0 engine at the head of a freight train, the 11.36 from Ludgershall waiting to follow us down to Westbury. By this point our speed has dropped below 50mph on the last mile at 1 in 106. Here the gradient turns to 1 in 132 down; indeed, it is downhill all the way to Westbury, so you can take your time about getting your fire back in order. Pressure is down to 210lb, but it soon comes up. The injector gradually refills the boiler. With less draught, as the engine is back to 17%, you can see what is happening in the firebox and can build a slight mound at the back, about half the area showing black. Then you sit down for the first time since Slough, pour out a mug of tea for you both and have a sandwich.

Past Wootton Rivers Halt, where the canal diverges to the north, Pewsey and Manningford Halt, we are really beginning to move. If you could rise and see the countryside like a map you would see 130 and 131, 10 miles apart, racing westwards at 85mph, the 8.30am Plymouth to Paddington express speeding the other way; three 'Kings'. To our left is a slope up to Salisbury Plain, with the Ridgeway on top of its windy heights, below it the road winding through a string of feudal villages, then the railway in great sweeping curves through the meadows. It is 12 noon and we are running on time.

You will recall a mention, at the start of our journey, of a slip guard. This gentleman is in charge of the two Weymouth coaches, isolated at the rear of the train, and now is time for his moment of glory. After passing the site of Edington & Bratton station and four following overbridges, he takes his post in the front of the slip coach. Here he has a handbrake and a lever which operates a brake application valve and a bolt, which latter retains the upper section of the drawhook. The lever has three positions. He pulls it back from Normal to Slip Brake On. The hook is released and hinges down, the vacuum hoses are jerked up, automatic sealing cocks close and they part, the vacuum brake is applied slightly on the slip portion and it drops back from the train. He winds the handbrake on and puts the lever forward to its middle position, Release. The vacuum brake is released by connecting the brake cylinders to a vacuum reservoir on the slip coach. The reservoir is big enough to give him two or three releases while retaining safe stopping power but since it cannot be replenished, it is good practice to use the handbrake as much as possible. Finally the coaches come silently to a halt alongside a pannier tank, standing on the up line, waiting to take them into Westbury.

You are not aware of what is happening at the back end, although the driver looks back to verify that the slip has detached. You are looking ahead, ready to make the next water pick-up from Fairwood trough. Westbury station is away to the right, a sprawl of yards and sheds surrounded by worked-out gravel pits, then the trough comes shortly beyond Fairwood Junction. That done, you look out for an occupation

Above: **Kennet & Avon Canal. In this prewar view No 6004** *King George III* **is hauling an express of 1938 stock. No details are on the print; the writer's guess for the location is Midgham.** *Great Western Railway*

Right: **A 'Grange' tearing past Fairwood Junction with a down express on 2 August 1952. The leading coach is 'Dreadnought' Brake Third No 3478 of 1905. The beginning of Fairwood water trough is visible in the distance. A curiosity is that the switched diamond in the junction is clearly set for the Westbury line.** *G. J. Jefferson*

crossing, then fire a couple of rounds. However, your mate gives a grunt of irritation, shuts off and slams the brake on. Hastily dropping the shovel, you turn to your window and see it too; Clink Road distant is on. The ATC squawks in agreement. The home signals come into view, but they don't move as they come closer and closer until they are right in front and you are practically stopped. The right-hand arm drops. You step across the cab, but your mate is already blowing the brake off and restarting her, and he points at the front window. Looking ahead under the bridge, you see the signalman at his door holding out a red flag. *KE* gives a few barks and then eases to a stop right beside him.

Line Blocked

At 11.45am the signalman at Blatchbridge Junction was looking at his instrument shelf, waiting for a track circuit indicator for Woodlands' intermediate block signal to switch from occupied to clear, thus unlocking his starter signal. The train in section was the 8.40am Class K freight from Bristol East depot to Weymouth, 28 wagons hauled by a 2-6-0 '4300' class engine. He was also waiting for Frome South box to request clearance to send on the 10.17am Bristol to Witham passenger train, a two-coach set with a pannier tank, which arrived at Frome at

Above left: **At Clink Road Jn before it was surrounded by roads and houses; a mixed freight hauled by 2-8-0 No 2847 trundles up the main line.** *Ivo Peters*

Below left: **'We've got a problem, Driver.'** *Ian Allan Library/LPC*

11.24 and was due to start at 11.49. When they reached Witham, both these trains were to shunt clear to allow train No 130 and its relief to pass.

What he got instead was a call on the telephone sited at the Woodlands signal. It was the freight train fireman, who said that they were stopped with a detached superheater element and could not move. Wouldn't it just have to happen in those few minutes when they were on the main line in front of the most important train of the day, but at least they were conveniently placed near a telephone and had lost no time in reporting the failure.

The Blatchbridge signalman immediately got on the telephone himself. He first informed Frome stationmaster, then used the all-stations circuit to advise his colleagues at Witham, Frome South, Frome North, Clink Road, Fairwood and Westbury South. The stationmaster acted with presence of mind sustained by a thorough knowledge of his patch and procedures. He realised at once that two expresses were coming

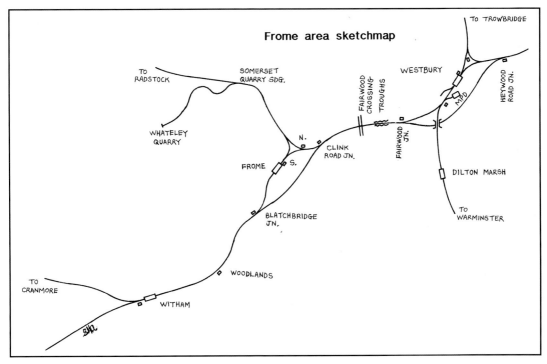

Frome area sketchmap

TO TROWBRIDGE

TO RADSTOCK

SOMERSET QUARRY SDG.

WESTBURY

HEYWOOD ROAD JN.

FAIRWOOD CROSSING TROUGHS

WHATELEY QUARRY

N.

CLINK ROAD JN.

FAIRWOOD JN.

FROME

S.

DILTON MARSH

BLATCHBRIDGE JN.

TO WARMINSTER

WOODLANDS

TO CRANMORE

WITHAM

towards him, and the quickest way of dealing with them would be to work them wrong line past the breakdown, and that to get them onto the up line, they must be brought into Frome station, where they could be reversed over a crossover. When he entered the South box, at the north end of the down platform, he found that the signalman was also thinking on the same lines. Such movements in Frome station are normal, for the triangular junction between North, South and West boxes is used for reversing Bristol & North Somerset line trains, involving propelling movements. He proposed to use the crossover at the north end of the station, as it has three important safety features: all the tracks near it are covered by track circuits, a signal is provided for the reversing movement, and the two sets of points over which the train would have to reverse are fitted with locks. Other points in the up line have no locks, so the yard staff were sent to secure them with hand clips (a device very like a carpenter's screw cramp) and stand by them with flags.

Fortunately, also, there was plenty of motive power available. This is a busy area, with heavy traffic from the limestone quarries serving the postwar building boom. Near Frome are Whateley and Vobster Quarries off the North Somerset line, and on the East Somerset line from Witham are Merehead and Dulcote Quarries, a Trinidad Lake Asphalt depot and Marcroft Wagons repair works at Cranmore. Frome has a pilot engine, housed overnight in the small engine shed there, which runs light to Westbury at 4.45am to bring the 5.20am goods back and is then employed shunting at Frome North and on trip workings to Somerset Quarry sidings on the branch, at 8.5am, 9.10am, 11.50am and 2.45pm. At the station there is a pilot available from 6am to 12.45pm, after which it departs with the 1.10pm passenger train to Bristol. The north end pilot is available at the station from 12.30pm to 2.30pm and a third pilot arrives at 7.22pm and shunts till 9.50 in the evening. More power is on hand at the locomotive depot at Westbury, which among

Above: **A pleasant interlude at Frome's little engine shed on 24 August 1956. Pannier tank No 4647 is probably the No 2 pilot, doing engine requirements before working to Bristol.** *H. C. Casserley*

Above right: **Frome North signalbox, built in 1880, is a typical example of a medium-size GWR box; Clink Road and Frome South were similar. This view shows it in its present form, rebuilt by the Great Western Society at Didcot Railway Centre, with its original name of Frome Mineral Junction.** *SHA*

Right: **A typical signalbox interior; Teignmouth on 9 June 1949. The signalman is pulling a lever, with a duster to avoid touching the polished handle. Everything in the box gleams, including, on the shelf, signal repeaters and the telegraph instruments and bells for communicating with Old Quay and Dawlish.** *E. D. Bruton*

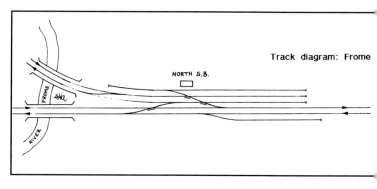

Track diagram: Frome

NORTH S.B.

FROME
SHED

RIVER

many duties has to keep an express passenger engine at immediate readiness to cover failures.

At Frome this morning, the south end pilot was promptly despatched to retrieve the stranded freight train and haul it back to here, while the north end pilot was ordered to leave his wagons and come down to the station. His task would be to pull the expresses over to the up road, a safer and quicker method than trying to push 13 coaches through a crossover. The staff tactfully extracted the passengers from the local train, which by good fortune had not yet started, asking them to wait for the next service; that train was then shunted into the down yard. By now train No 130 was approaching Heywood Road; the decision to allow it to run at full speed right up to Clink Road and thus make its normal water pick-up was a welcome, and some might say rare, touch of appreciation by the signalmen of the practicalities of the steam engine. Five minutes later both roads through the station were clear, with the north end pilot tucked into the down loop behind the box.

At 12.12 the 10.33am Weymouth to Wolverhampton passenger train came into the station. Its driver was able to confirm the location of the disabled freight. Just as it was starting away, the majestic 'Cornish Riviera Limited' rolled in from the opposite direction.

While all this activity to keep traffic moving was taking place at a local level, the massive structure of railway management must of course be allowed to join in — or in railway jargon, Rule 177 must be applied. After the first discussions the signalman called his Signal Department Lineman at Westbury, his Inspector at Bristol and the Westbury Control Office. Westbury Control in turn advised a clutch of District Officers: the Traffic Superintendent, Operating Assistant, Commercial Assistant, Chief Inspector, Running & Maintenance Officer, Engineer and Signal Department Inspector. No doubt orders would in due time come down from these exalted levels concerning the incident, and with any luck the

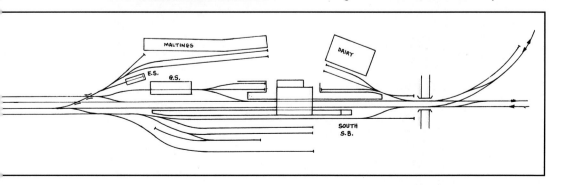

problem would be dealt with satisfactorily before that happened.

King Edward II has drawn to a stand at Clink Road Junction and the signalman tells you that you are to go into Frome and work single line wrong road to Witham. He then holds up a green flag and *KE* barks away through the cutting, past Frome North, over the river and into the station. Frome North only lowers his home signal when we are near it and holds out a green flag, this being a warning under Block Signalling Regulation 5 that there is an obstruction ahead. You shut your dampers and turn on the live steam injector, but with a sudden cessation in the demand for steam it is not many minutes before the boiler is full and the safety valves start to blow.

Incidentally, it may occur to you that had this happened at Heywood Road, it would have been impossible to release the slip portion. Quite right; if the slip guard had not seen that the signals were off, he would not have pulled the lever.

Frome station is notable, though not unusual for 1957, for having its Brunel timber roof intact. It was built in 1850 and was for six years a terminus until the line was extended to Yeovil. The original timber station now sits astride the much-extended platforms. It has a short bay platform on the up side but that is of little use because of sharp curves; 70ft coaches are barred from it and the Express Dairy siding. At the south end are a goods shed, dock and livestock siding, and a newer goods depot on the down side. The yard is dominated by the handsome range of Bailey's Maltings. (A malt house is a heated store where grain is germinated before being made into beer.) This busy country town even forms the starting point for a through train to London, at 8.15am.

To clear the points at rear, your engine has to pass the platform starter signal and run as far as

Above left: **The location of the freight train breakdown in this narrative. Woodlands box was just beyond the trees on the right. In the background is Roddenbury Hill. This photograph was taken in 1996 and shows the contemporary practice of burying the sleepers in ballast.** *SHA*

Above centre: **The twin viaducts over the River Frome at Frome North Jn. The main line has been rebuilt with a plate girder structure; the North Somerset Viaduct is the original.** *SHA*

Above right: **Frome's historic timber station building, looking north from the down platform in September 1966.** *A. Muckley*

Right: **Frome station in July 1996, from the up platform. The down platform and waiting room were closed off and disused.** *SHA*

the down yard points; the stationmaster has anticipated this as well and has come down to show you where to stop. You rumble through the roof, past a few spectators who materialise at a country station when anything unusual occurs, and a gaggle of passengers; the authorities helpfully refused to allow 130 to take them up, so they are joining your train. Your mate stops her, puts his brake handle to Running and waits. After a couple of minutes the vacuum rises of its own accord, showing that the pannier tank has coupled on, and this is confirmed by a distant crow whistle, which you repeat. Your mate cracks the regulator just enough to open the jockey valve, so that the engine takes her own weight as you run back. The stationmaster rides with you, stopping the movement with a red flag, after which he gets off and is replaced by someone else. After some more conferring, which you cannot hear because she is still

blowing off vigorously, you see from your side the signalman holding a green flag from his box window, so you call across, 'Green from the box.'

'We're right away then,' replies your mate, and starts her up.

Now, running trains the wrong way along one line of a double line is potentially a very dangerous business; there is no system for preventing conflicting movements as there is on single lines. Although the signalmen have agreed what is intended, further safeguards are

prescribed, and you will not be surprised to learn that they take the form of paperwork.

The engine going out to rescue the stranded freight carries a Wrong Line Order Form D, issued by the signalman to allow it to return on the down line to Frome. It stops at Blatchbridge to have the form countersigned by the signalman there. (There are other Wrong Line Orders: 'A' is issued by a guard to allow the engine to return to his train from the signalbox ahead, 'B' is issued by a driver to allow another engine to approach him from the box ahead and 'C' is issued by a guard to allow the driver to reverse the front part of a divided train towards the rear part.) A pilotman is appointed who must accompany, or despatch, every train through the temporary single line and who issues Single Line Working forms to all stationmasters and signalmen concerned, carrying a form himself which the others all sign. Not until he has collected up and cancelled all the forms may normal working be resumed. There are also detailed rules as to how the signals must be worked and the Block Signalling Regulations applied.

Today the Witham stationmaster decided that, as the 10.33am from Weymouth was already at his station, he would act as pilotman himself, riding on it to Frome and delivering his single line forms. He then instructed 130 to proceed and is now riding on your engine back to Witham. He will subsequently ride the next up train, the 6.25am Penzance to Paddington (the first train out of Penzance in the morning), which will have to divert into Frome, and the next down, the 11.45am Chippenham to Weymouth, and so on until the down line is cleared.

Your driver runs at a moderate speed, blowing the whistle at frequent intervals. You are worried about what is happening to your fire. The chief problem when a big fire loses its draught is that the iron and sulphur content of the coal, instead of being dispersed, melts and collects in the lowest part, where air coming up from beneath solidifies it. It may bind the bottom layer of cinders into a solid sheet on the firebars. In a word, clinker. Once under way again, you take up the long pricker, taking care not to hit the bridge at Blatchbridge, and rake the fire as deeply as you can, sliding it between almost closed doors. Open up the front dampers. On finishing, you look' out to see a pannier tank

Right: **Wrong Line Order Form D.** *Author's collection*

Below: **Wrong Line Order Chart.** *Author's collection*

ORDER	In possession of and issued by	Issued to	Retained by	Countersigned by	Cancelled Order retained by	Lights carried moving in wrong direction	Lights carried when drawn back	Lights carried when propelled forward
A	GUARD	SIGNALMAN	SIGNALMAN	SIGNALMAN / DRIVER OF ASSISTING ENGINE if any	GUARD	TRAIN ENGINE PRESCRIBED HEAD CODE	WHITE LIGHT ON LEADING VEHICLE / RED TAIL LIGHT	WHITE LIGHT ON LEADING VEHICLE / PROPELLING ENGINE RED TAIL LIGHT
B	DRIVER	SIGNALMAN	SIGNALMAN	SIGNALMAN	DRIVER			TRAIN ENGINE PRESCRIBED HEAD CODE / ASSISTING ENGINE RED TAIL LIGHT
C	GUARD	DRIVER	DRIVER	SIGNALMAN / DRIVER OF ASSISTING ENGINE if any	GUARD	PRESCRIBED HEAD CODE / TRAIN RED TAIL LIGHTS		
D	SIGNALMAN	DRIVER	SIGNALMAN	SIGNALMAN	SIGNALMAN		TRAIN ENGINE PRESCRIBED HEAD CODE / ASSISTING ENGINE RED TAIL LIGHT	

moving slowly ahead on the other line, and at that moment there is a puff of smoke from under its front wheels, followed by a bang. He has hit one of the detonators put down by the freight train guard.

A detonator is a large version of the caps you fired in your toy gun when playing cowboys and Indians: a few ounces of gunpowder in a light metal case 1½in in diameter, with strips attached which you bend round the rail head to hold it. It is exploded by the impact of a wheel. You will appreciate that it is dangerous to be near it when it goes off, because of flying shards of metal. Actually, that other crew are lucky, for if they had hit that 'shot' as your train was passing, almost certainly with people looking out of the windows to see what was happening, the effect could have been nasty. Whistle up to warn them, and again when you see the stationary train with its engine now helpless at the far end. Here at last is Witham station, where you must stop to put down the extra passengers and the pilotman. Handsignalmen are in position at the clipped-up points.

Witham has a curiosity, a little timber roof over the bay platform where East Somerset trains arrive. There is no run-round; coaches are shunted back up the branch and run down past their engine by gravity. Down branch trains have to start from the down main line.

The single line operation has been an achievement of some 20 railwaymen, pulling together as a team, using the full depth of their experience and breadth of their knowledge, but the fact remains that you are 20 minutes behind schedule.

Top right: **A view through the cab window of a pannier tank hauling a branch line train on the East Somerset line. The difficulty of seeing anything close in front, on an engine intended for shunting, is apparent. This photograph and the next were taken with the help of the East Somerset Railway.** *SHA*

Above: **The pannier tank coming onto the back of our train.** *SHA*

Right: **Protecting a train by placing a detonator on the rail. (Taken with the help of the Bluebell Railway.)** *SHA*

Clear Road West

Getting the right-away, *KE* lurches uneasily over the crossover to the west of the platforms, and you watch your train as it follows over. Your driver opens up to full regulator and 35%, and all the metaphors about gunshots or what have you are inadequate to convey the voice of a 'King' in full cry. I'm afraid you just have to be there. And being there, you have to get shovelling. She belts like a mountain goat up the 1 in 107 to Brewham box, between Downs Farm and Bellerica Farm on the watershed separating the Frome and the Brue. It is as well that the breakdown did not happen here, for there are catch points on the rising gradients and someone would have had to come out and close them for wrong-line working. Not a very high summit, just under 400ft above sea level, but the start of a 23-mile descent to Sedgemoor, the average gradient working out at 1 in 320.

Normally you can expect to sit down for a while here, keeping a good lookout for Sheephouse Farm crossing, and have your lunch. Today, however, although your mate winds the reverser back a little, he doesn't turn it nearly as much as you would like, and the glare from above the flap is like an arc-light. You have to keep feeding her as she screams down through Castle Cary (the station whose goods shed was felled by a bomb in 1942, either by luck or very good aiming), and the village stations of Keinton Mandeville and Charlton Mackrell. These little stations slumber in the heart of Somerset farmland, disturbed only by the Castle Cary to

Above left: **At Brewham Summit on a typical English summer day, 29 July 1961, 'Hall' No 4909** *Blakesley Hall* **brings a Weymouth-Paddington train up from Bruton. The camera is looking south and Brewham is over a mile away on the far side of the hill.** *G. A. Richardson*

Left: **What a coincidence, and the photographer was there to capture it. No 7029** *Clun Castle,* **climbing Brewham Bank from the west, reaches the Somerset & Dorset line crossing at Cole just as S&D 2-8-0 No 53805 goes over, at about 2pm on 13 August 1960. The S&D train is identified as the 12.26pm Bournemouth-Nottingham.** *G. A. Richardson*

Taunton auto train, four times a day each way. Flyaway expresses like ours have nothing to say to them. The engine is dancing about a little, but the really alarming thing is the way the bushes are whipping by your open cabside, giving you an unpleasant feeling of being airborne. The wide curve round Kingsdown Hill looks like a street corner. As you flick up the flap your mate grabs your sleeve.

'Something to tell your grandchildren.' He points at the little speedometer in front of him. It is reading 105.

'Nah, they'd never believe me.'

Thanks to those fitters in Swindon and their fine-finished axleboxes, to the erecting shop men with their telescopic alignment jigs, and to the permanent way men for this track on which there is no speed limit, you might believe it. But this sort of thing cannot go on for ever. At Athelney (educational note — on your right is where King Alfred burnt the cakes) he shuts off, so speed has decayed to a civilised level as you join the four-track section at Cogload Junction, and you are able to make a pick-up from Creech trough. Just after that you get Taunton East distant on. In fact, you have caught up 130, and its driver would be quite surprised if he knew that you have managed it with a single-chimney 'King' while he has a double one.

At Cogload the lines to and from Bristol take position either side of ours, and are now designated as relief lines, ours being the main lines. Alongside on the left is another express train, headed by a 'Castle', coming to a stand at signals. That is the 'Cornishman', 9.0am Wolverhampton to Penzance, the train which is scheduled to follow us all the way from here.

Taunton was a major recipient of the 1929 finance, when the four tracks from Cogload to Norton Fitzwarren were put in, the station rebuilt and the yards extended. The marshalling yards at Fairwater and Blinkhorn were laid down during the war. The station is a train watcher's delight, being a terminus for services on all seven radiating routes. To its north is the Great Western's concrete works. South of the station is an engine shed, where one of the events inspiring the feature film *The Titfield Thunderbolt* occurred: 0-4-2 tank No 5812 got away by

herself and smashed through the wall above the street, fortunately in reality without going any farther. (A few years later this same engine succeeded in taking to the highway at Chard Junction.)

Trains 130 and 131 are among the very few to run through Taunton without stopping. Passing through the platform your driver consults his watch. The 27½ miles from Castle Cary have taken 22 minutes, an average speed of 75mph and five minutes less than schedule.

This is unfamiliar ground to you, but you do know that there is a big hill coming up. It starts easily enough, through the Tone meadows and the complex junction of Norton Fitzwarren. Then it steepens to 1 in 174 past Poole Siding to Wellington, then 1 in 90, 86, and 80 up to Whiteball Tunnel. You do not need your mate to tell you, he is going to give her a real hammering. As you pause for a gulp of tea and to catch the Wellington signals you see him glance across at you, but you give him a grin. Sweat is stinging in your eyes. You work like blazes to get and keep a thick fire, right up to the firehole rim. If you were not physically fit you couldn't do it. On the steep part she is beating you, coal just shoots off

the shovel in the pull of the blast and you have no idea where it is going, and steam is falling back past 210lb. The engine is rocking to her piston thrusts, quivering from the big end impacts. Inside the tunnel the din makes your ears smart. It is preposterous to think that one little man can control 90 tons of shrieking steel with a white-hot heart; you are just clinging to the back of her like a monkey on a liberty horse.

Daylight returns and she races away down the hill, but at least the engine is eased, allowing you to take stock; your fire is a lumpy mess, you have less than half a glass of water and your steam is below 200lb, but what the heck, you have had enough. You sit down. The train gathers speed down the bank past Burlescombe, a little place destined to make history in the future, when a piece of the supposedly extinct broad gauge track is discovered buried in the Westleigh Lime & Stone Co quarry. A 'King' roars past the other way — the 9.30am Falmouth to Paddington. Glancing at the gauge glass, you are puzzled to see that the level has gone up; the injector has been on since Taunton and you had ceased to notice it. You are the only one who is hot and bothered; the engine is humming along with a

Left: **The 11.25am Cardiff-Penzance, hauled by 'Castle' No 5059** *Earl St Aldwyn,* **gathers speed on the descent from Whiteball Tunnel. By the signalbox are the crew of 2-6-2T No 4136, awaiting orders after assisting a train from Wellington. The right-hand pair of signals, at danger, are for a running goods loop which begins behind the camera and extends to Burlescombe. The date is 4 September 1954.** *R. C. Riley*

Right: **'Grange' No 6809** *Burghclere Grange* **drifting downhill at Eastbrook, midway between Whiteball and Burlescombe, with a Class H unbraked freight train, on 17 August 1960.** *M. J. Fox*

contented purr at the chimney and the air pump ticking merrily, your mate is unconcerned. He beckons you over to take his seat while he goes into the tender to answer a call of nature, a procedure you will not find in any manual.

Having another look in the fire, you realise that the front of it has disappeared. Using the short pricker you push the back over and also pull some coal down the tender. After that you partially close the dampers, turn off the injector and whang a couple of dozen good shovelfuls down the front and along the sides. In a few minutes the pressure is going the right way. We are passing Hele, still cruising at nearly 90mph, and shoot past a goods train shunting into Wiggins Teape's paper mill. The driver's hand shifts to the brake lever, holds it over until the brake is well on, then back upright; then on again, and the ATC squawks in unison. Here is the River Exe, the narrow pass between Pynes and the green bank of Stoke Woods, round the bend to the Cowley Bridge Inn. A small signalbox nestles between railway and river, controlling the vital junction where Southern and Western meet. Through a bridge arch, we come to the reception lines of Riverside Yard. We are now looking south towards the sun; towards England's Riviera, and the sea.

Exeter St David's station is where the West Country really starts. Whether it is the smell of tidal water, for Exeter is a port, or an extra brightness in the air, or the informality of cars and carts crossing the lines right under the noses of the Southern banking engines, or the setting so rural for such a big station; whatever it is that signifies pleasure in life, this station has it. As we run in, on our right is Riverside Yard, another wartime development; from there, goods lines extend round the outside of the older goods station, leaving it confined between them and the main lines. Sidings on the down side are restricted by a steep hillside. The passenger station provides one down and two up platforms and a down through road, the central island platform being used mostly by Southern trains and locals to Torbay. Banking engines for the incline to Central stand by in a short siding between the main lines by Exeter Middle box. At the southwest corner, just above the river — or in wet weather just below it — lies the locomotive depot. At the south end are two survivors from the early history of the South Devon Railway: a timber carriage shed and the atmospheric-system pump house, now part of the railway gasworks.

At 25mph *KE* noses her way into the down main road and drifts through, just as the up 'Cornish Riviera' runs through in the opposite direction. The boys on the platform do not know which way to look. It is 1.50pm and we are a quarter of an hour late.

Although in the timetable 130 is supposed to be 20 minutes ahead of 131, it is now only four sections farther down, passing Exminster, and with speed limits all the way there will be little more racing on this trip. Your engine rolls through St David's and over two bridges, the second built in 1938 as part of an expansion scheme for the station which never took place. Below a hill crowned with the bulk of Exeter Cathedral, we pass through St Thomas, which, had it not been for the Frome incident, would be the first original Brunel trainshed we encountered on the main line. The waterway now on our left is the Exeter Canal, the oldest artificial canal in the country. It leads out to Countess Wear, where Powderham Castle guards the broadening estuary.

Just after Exminster station comes the last water trough. The pick-up is easy at 55mph and you fill her up. By firing little and often you have

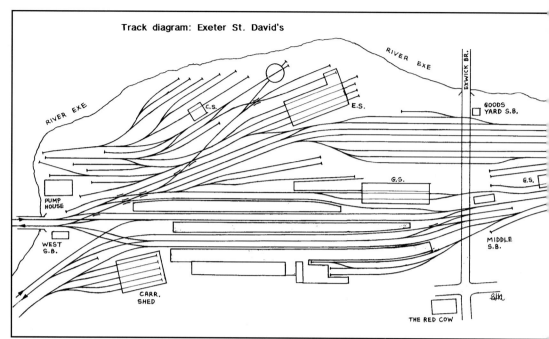

Track diagram: Exeter St. David's

RIVER EXE

RIVER EXE

EXWICK BR.

GOODS YARD S.B.

C.S.

E.S.

G.S.

G.S.

PUMP HOUSE

MIDDLE S.B.

WEST S.B.

CARR. SHED

THE RED COW

25

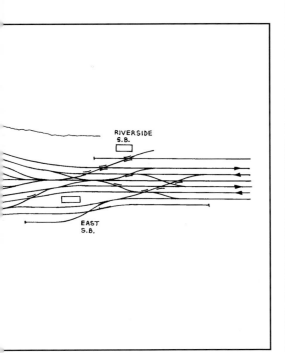

RIVERSIDE
S.B.

EAST
S.B.

an adequate bed of fire, three-quarters of a glass and 250lb on the clock, so you build a mound on the back of the grate with a saddle to enable you to see over to the front, then clean up the footplate and brew a fresh can of tea. The coal supply is much depleted and you have to pull some more forward. Tired? After a mere three hours' bending and lifting in front of a furnace?

On the up line the mid-morning return loads of holidaymakers are coming by: the 12.15 Kingswear to Wolverhampton, 10.30 Penzance to Wolverhampton and 10.5 Penzance to Manchester pass in quick succession. At Dawlish Warren the beach comes to join us and we lean into the curve through Langstone Rock and come out on the sea wall. Dawlish, that genteel resort, grumbled when the railway was built along its frontage, but they have cause to be thankful now that they do not have a motor road there. Ahead the red cliffs slope down to sparkling sea, blue as only Devon sea can be. Under easy steam your 'King' strolls along through the short tunnels, past Sprey Point, acknowledging human strollers with regal condescension, round Teignmouth East Cliff and through the town.

From your seat you can enjoy a little social analysis: on Dawlish front, respectable couples in print, piping and parasols take their leisure as they have done since *KE* was new, and the Blenheim Private Hotel offers 'H&C in all Bedrooms and Separate Tables'; whereas round by the Warren are the postwar generation of

Far left: **Cowley Bridge Junction, looking north from the road bridge. The Southern line crosses the River Exe to head up into North Devon. The impressive bundle of rods and wires coming from the box controls not only this junction but also the connections to the Riverside goods lines, to the south on the other side of the bridge.** *M. J. Fox*

Above: **There are few man-made objects in the landscape as pretty as an array of GWR signals; this is the Exeter Middle down main home.** *SHA*

Below: **Exeter Middle signalbox, adjoining Red Cow level crossing. It stands between tracks in a narrow space, so the huge locking frame has to be mounted vertically and the cabin overhangs it to give the men room to work. The road trailer bearing the emblem of National Carriers Ltd gives away the period of this view, taken on 28 August 1978.** *G. Scott-Lowe*

families, young and hatless, for whom the Golden Sands Camp provides 'Electric and Radio and Recreation Room'. When standing on a tender in driving sleet you have often longed for a stuffy factory job, but a day like this when Heaven smiles on your green engine makes up for all the rest. After Teignmouth you open your dampers and give her a touch of blower.

At the head of the Teign Estuary appear a broad and busy marshalling yard, a spacious station, sheds and workshops, decorated with plumes of steam here and there. Newton Abbot! How many boys would be happy if their holiday took them no further than this feast of colour, sound and movement. Twice round the clock in summer, trains are being divided or joined, engines are being changed and the running shed and factory are busy. The former South Devon shops still thrive, sufficiently far from Swindon to preserve a degree of independence to the extent that after 10 years of Nationalisation they are still painting engines in GWR green. The legacy of the atmospheric railway also gives Newton the status of a frontier town, for to the east lie 20 miles of level while westwards are the mountainous grades of West Devon and Cornwall.

The station presents a crowded appearance, for the 1.10pm Kingswear to Exeter and the Moretonhampstead branch train, both headed by

Above: **As we run into Exeter St David's we see an Exe Valley auto-train at the middle platform. The engine is the famous No 1466, whose preservation was the first achievement of the Great Western Society. On the right is No 34002** *Salisbury,* **the engine which worked the last BR steam train to Penzance.** *IA Library*

Above right: **Summer Saturday in South Devon. A 13-coach train passes Dawlish Warren and rounds the curve through Langstone Rock to the sea wall. The engine is express freight 2-8-0 No 4700, commandeered to help with the holiday rush. The train is the 8.0am Manchester-Penzance, on 16 July 1955.** *R. C. Riley*

Right: **This photograph of the 'Limited' at Langstone Rock on 9 August 1956 is annotated that the train was over an hour late, and that the engine No 6822** *Manton Grange* **was based at Westbury. It is likely that she took over from a failed 'King' somewhere in Somerset.** *T. E. Williams*

'5100' class 2-6-2Ts, are due to start at 2.15pm and are about to go. The St Philips Marsh '2800' which brought the 3.0am freight from Severn Tunnel Junction has cut off its train in Hackney Yard and is running forward through the Graveyard Sidings towards the depot. At 2.17pm 131 pulls up on the down relief platform. Nearby,

Above left: Up coal empties, hauled by 2-8-0 No 2861, on the sea wall on 30 May 1949. It is passing Parsons Tunnel down home signal; Teignmouth down distant is just beyond the tail of the train. The cliffs along here were completely reshaped by the railway engineers; originally they were almost vertical. *E. D. Bruton*

Left: The up 'Limited', the 1956 BR set hauled by No 6017 *King Edward IV*, in final form with double chimney, cruising along the sea wall from Teignmouth to Sprey Point. In the down line by the front of the engine is a flange lubricator: a gadget like a grease-gun which deposits a little thick graphite grease on passing wheel flanges, with the idea that it spreads out and reduces wear when the flanges touch the rail on sharp curves. *R. C. Riley*

Above: Eastcliff Bridge, Teignmouth, is a 'must include', and we have chosen an unusual subject: LMS '8F' 2-8-0 No 48424 with an up Class F unbraked fast freight. As usual, a family waves to the fireman. *S. Creer*

Below: Locomotive coal supplies for Newton Abbot approaching Hackney; the fireman is looking out for the signal, and we can see that the train is signalled into the yard. The bridge is on the road from Kingsteignton to the Passage House Inn. The engine is 2-8-0 No 3814, which has had the good fortune to be preserved. *J. R. Besley*

the nerve centre of operations is a small hut, identifiable by a blue haze above it when trains are running late, containing an inspector whose job is to conduct an orchestra whose players all think they have been given the wrong instrument. On the platform beside it is a group of enginemen, either ready to relieve or just relieved, indulging in the humorous, mock-aggressive banter that arises wherever an élite are gathered together. Two of them, who are going to work your assisting engine to Plymouth, come over to your cab, together with a cleaner from the shed to push your coal forward. Doing that on a succession of tenders for a day in the sun is a punishing job for a boy of 17 and helps to weed out those who haven't got what it takes.

The pilot is already backing on, 'Grange' No 6849 *Walton Grange*. A station inspector is on hand to note this and hurry back to inform your guard. No sooner is the vacuum coupled up than a blast of steam comes from the pilot's chimney as he blows the brake off, the down relief to main starter drops and within three minutes we are under way again, both engines blowing off as they accelerate briskly under the bridge.

Four tracks are provided as far as Aller Junction, where the Torbay line goes straight on and the main line curves right. There is a down refuge loop here, and we are not the only ones running late; it is occupied by a freight train with engines front and rear. By now you have enough in the box, and turn the blower off and shut the doors for the ascent of Dainton. With ample pulling power the bank is no great problem, but the music is lovely and you are content to lean on your side sheet to listen.

Slowly now, hammering out the beat, nosing from side to side, our pair clamber up to the level

Below: 'Grange' No 6813 *Eastbury Grange* crossing the Teign Bridge from Hackney to Newton Abbot with an express in July 1958. *D. S. Fish*

Right: A view from Newton Abbot East box at about 1.20pm on 18 July 1956. The engine wheeling the up 'Limited' out is No 6015 *King Richard III*. The South Devon Railway works lie on the far left. Shunting carriages in the centre is pannier tank No 8404, one of those which were transferred in the following November to the Lickey Incline. Another up train is waiting to start. *R. C. Riley*

Below Right: On 25 July 1962, a relief to the 3.0pm Plymouth-Cardiff was run from Newton Abbot. 'Hall' No 4996 *Eden Hall* brings the empty train into the up platform. The short platform on the right is used by Moretonhampstead branch trains and has its own public entrance. *J. S. Whiteley*

Right: **A view which exemplifies the atmosphere at Newton Abbot on a Saturday afternoon. Train 328, the 9.5am Swansea-Kingswear, hauled by a BR '9F' 2-10-0, has the road; train No 329, the 9.25am Wolverhampton-Kingswear, hauled by a 'Castle', waits its turn; train No 428, the 9.0am Wolverhampton-Penzance, hauled by another 'Castle', waits for an assisting engine, which has been signalled on by the ground discs; No 4976** *Warfield Hall* **stands on the coaches of a local; a pannier tank is south end pilot; and 'Manor' No 7820** *Dinmore Manor* **comes off the locomotive depot.** *D. S. Fish*

Above: **At Newton Abbot at 2.40pm on 4 April 1961. A diesel locomotive on the down 'Limited' failed and was replaced by No 6874** *Haughton Grange,* **which reached Newton nearly 1hr late. The fireman removes his headlamps ready for the 'Hall' in the background, No 4905** *Barton Hall,* **to back on.**

Alongside in the up platform is the Ashburton branch freight, hauled by 2-6-2T No 4555. *J. R. Besley*

Below: **Newton Abbot engine shed in September 1959. 2-8-0 No 2875 has received the attention of the cleaners, unlike the 'Hall' behind her.** *D. S. Fish*

of Stoneycombe Quarry. The roar echoing round the countryside is abruptly muffled as they plunge into Dainton Tunnel at about 25mph. Your mate stands in the middle of the cab drinking tea and only moves as the tunnel comes up to ease the regulator and turn the blower on. You are enveloped in a fog so thick that you can see nothing except the flashes of light from the slit between the firedoors. You know you are out of the tunnel by the sound, but it takes longer before the mist clears and green South Devon is back, showing on your left and ahead when the tender in front leans away to the right.

Faster and faster down the bank until the vacuum needle drops and the brake is felt checking your career into the Dart Valley. Braking is done entirely by the man in front, your ejectors being off and the brake handle in running position. Of course the air pump is still working but when train pipe vacuum falls below 22in a shuttle valve switches it from sucking from the train pipe to sucking from the engine reservoir, so that it helps rather than hinders the braking. Meanwhile, you black the fire out again and start both injectors. With only 25 miles to go, you must take thought to running your fire down, so as not to arrive on shed with a great mass which would go to waste. As soon as Totnes is out of the way and she is blasting up the 1 in 66 to Tigley you

ask your mate about it. He has a look in the box for himself.

'No more on after Rattery.' He pauses. 'You've done a fair bit today lad.'

Praise indeed.

You bend your back for one last session, launching four to the front, rolling four down the sides, dropping four on the back, flick up the flap, wait till the smoke clears, do it again, until you have cleared the coal you had 'in the hole' at the tender front. The train is roaring through Marley Tunnel, still uphill, but for two engines on this load it is easy going. On your right is Brent Hill, an actual mountain, just over 1,000ft; an outlier of the great waste of Dartmoor, whose bare shoulders crowd in close. On the easier gradients towards South Brent speed rises to the 50mph limit, and so does your pressure until she is blowing off again. Your mate gives her another notch for the last bit. The summit is at Wrangaton station, at 455ft above sea level.

You partially close your dampers and turn on both injectors to raise the water level as she tilts down the way, and a puff of steam from under the 'Grange's' footplate shows that he has done the same. Next we pass, stopped at Bittaford Platform, a 'square' engine, a Southern 'West Country' working the 2.15pm from Plymouth. That is one of the turns booked for Southern and

Above: **On the level between Newton Abbot and Aller Jn, the 10.35 gathers speed on 17 September 1955. The train engine, No 6021** *King Richard II,* **brought it down from London. The leading engine, No 6009** *King Charles II,* **brought the 10.30 down and is still carrying the number and headboard, which should have been removed at Newton.** *Ian Allan Library/LPC*

Left: **Aller Jn in high summer, 4 August 1956. The Torbay line goes straight ahead and the main line, with the down goods loop just visible, curves right. The two engines, No 6978** *Haroldstone Hall* **and No 5941** *Campion Hall,* **have been prepared at Newton Abbot to work up holiday expresses from Torbay, and are taking some empty stock down.**
Ian Allan Library

Below left: **Climbing Dainton Bank. The subject is identified as the 9.30am Paddington-Falmouth on 12 December 1959, engine No 5008** *Raglan Castle. J. B. Smith*

Above: **The train is not specified here but it could well be 131. Nos 5934** *Kneller Hall* **and 6015** *King Richard III* **are on the steep pitch of Dainton, approaching the tunnel, on 15 August 1957. The fireman on the 'King' appears to be having trouble with his injector.** *A. C. Cawston*

Right: **A curious combination of motive power is found on the 12.20pm Penzance-Kensington milk train on 29 June 1957: No 6986** *Rydal Hall* **leading 2-8-0 No 3832. They are passing the box and sidings at Dainton Summit. The sidings are level, the main line falls at 1 in 118.** *R. C. Riley*

Left: **This unidentified photograph shows either the 10.30 or the 10.35 coming down through Totnes. Judging by the filthy state of No 6007** *King William III* **and the train engine, it is in the last years. On the left is the 2.15pm Plymouth-Exeter, hauled by a Southern Region 'West Country'.** *Ian Allan Library*

Below: **A golden evening in the last summer of the 1930s. The 3.30pm Paddington-Truro passes Tigley box, where the gradient eases from 1 in 52 to 1 in 74, in June 1939; engine No 6022** *King Edward III.* **Engine, train, permanent way, lineside — everything is immaculate.** *H. K. Harman*

Above: **Another scene at Tigley box, on 7 September 1957. The unusual summer Saturday train which started from Ealing Broadway at 7.25am for Penzance is hauled by No 4075** *Cardiff Castle* **and assisted by 'Manor' No 7814** *Fringford Manor.*
A. R. Butcher

Right: **The 2.15pm Plymouth-Exeter, worked by a Southern crew to keep up their familiarity with the route, at Cornwood Viaduct, seen from the lane down to Woodburn. On 10 April 1954 it is hauled by No 34016** *Bodmin.* **A milk van brings up the rear.**
D. S. Fish

Below right: **On the morning of 5 August 1956 the Saturday 5.30pm through train from Glasgow St Enoch, due in Plymouth at 11.55 on Sunday morning, passes Hemerdon box. No 7814** *Fringford Manor* **pilots No 5027** *Farleigh Castle.* **A freight, headed by LMS 2-8-0 No 48410, probably purloined after taking a cross-London trip to Southall, has been put into the loop to allow it to pass.** *R. J. Blenkinsop*

Western crews over each other's routes, so that they are all current on both and can be diverted onto the other line if the sea wall or the heights of Meldon are blocked by winter weather. Which happens more often is according to one's loyalty.

In relative quiet, with just a breath of steam on, we swing easily along the moor side, high above the town of Ivybridge. Sometimes all is hidden by a cutting, then we are looking down at the treetops as we glide over one of the streams that scamper down off the moor; sometimes on a little bridge, sometimes on a major viaduct as at Cornwood or Ivybridge where speed has to be checked. You loosen your fire with the pricker, wash down the floor and tender front, turn off the injector and finish your tea in time to sit down and enjoy the ride down Hemerdon bank. A minute or two later it occurs to you to draw a pail of water and wash your face and hands; it

would never do for anyone, most of all your friend on 130, to see you finish your first Plymouth job looking hot and dirty.

Down in Plymouth, train No 130's late arrival is causing some muttering among thinly reconciled rivals. It is due to run in between two Southern trains, the 2.15pm Plymouth Friary to Waterloo and the 2.25pm to Exeter, but (and you do not find this out until later) the second of these was first held at Friary, then let go. Then they found that the 1.47pm from Newton Abbot had been put in front of 130 and was slightly early. It was stopped at Laira Junction and was barely cleared in time to avoid stopping 130. By the time you arrive, London trains are not popular. For timetable enthusiasts, a list follows of the trains scheduled to be on the section from Lipson Junction to Devonport Junction between 2.0 and 2.30pm, with their booked times at North Road.

11.0am Penzance-Paddington	Arr 1.52	Dep 2.0
1.55pm transfer trip		
Devonport Albert Rd Goods-Tavistock Jn	Pass 2.3	
9.30am Paddington-Falmouth/Newquay	Arr 2.0	Dep 2.8
2.15pm Plymouth NR-Exeter St David's	Arr 2.9 ecs from Millbay	Dep 2.15
		(worked by SR engine)
1.25pm Saltash-Tavistock South auto	Dep 2.10	
1.55pm Saltash-Plymouth auto	Arr 2.11	
2.15pm Plymouth-Saltash auto	Dep 2.15	
11.0am Exeter Riverside-Laira via SR freight	Pass 2.17	
12.30pm Doublebois-Laira freight	Pass 2.20	
2.15pm Plymouth Friary-Waterloo	Arr 2.23	Dep 2.25
11.47am Exeter Central-Plymouth Friary	Arr 2.23	Dep 2.28
		(worked by WR engine)
10.30am Paddington-Penzance	Arr 2.30	
2.25pm Plymouth Friary-Exeter Central	Arr 2.33	Dep 2.35
		(worked by WR engine)

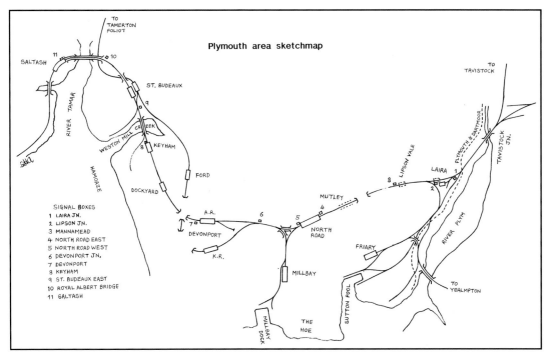

Plymouth area sketchmap

TO TAMERTON FOLIOT

SALTASH

RIVER TAMAR

TAMAR

HAMOAZE

ST. BUDEAUX

WESTON MILL CREEK

KEYHAM

FORD

DOCKYARD

A.R.

DEVONPORT

K.R.

MILLBAY

MILLBAY DOCK

THE HOE

SUTTON POOL

MUTLEY

NORTH ROAD

FRIARY

LIPSON VALE

LAIRA

PLYMOUTH & DARTMOOR

RIVER PLYM

TAVISTOCK JN.

TO TAVISTOCK

TO YEALMPTON

SIGNAL BOXES
1 LAIRA JN.
2 LIPSON JN.
3 MANNAMEAD
4 NORTH ROAD EAST
5 NORTH ROAD WEST
6 DEVONPORT JN.
7 DEVONPORT
8 KEYHAM
9 ST. BUDEAUX EAST
10 ROYAL ALBERT BRIDGE
11 SALTASH

Above left: **A down freight moves out onto the main line from Tavistock Jn yard on 17 November 1956; engine No 6809** *Burghclere Grange. R. T. Roxon*

Below: **Laira Jn on 30 August 1961. A down freight, hauled by No 6873** *Caradoc Grange,* **conveying a dozen china clay wagons with their tarpaulins, passes on the main line. The Plymouth & Dartmoor Railway comes down the slope above the wagons, through the white gate and across immediately behind the signalbox.** *R. C. Riley*

Plymouth is the only urban sprawl in the whole West Country. It is nearly three times the size of Exeter and 10 times as big as any Cornish town. It has its mean streets, and living in a terrace house in a mean street is pretty much the same everywhere. However, where the local stone is used its light colour brings an air of brightness and cleanliness to the place, and it is swept by sea air. It also has by far the finest shopping centre in Britain. From Pennycomequick Hill to the Hoe extends a network of broad walks and new buildings where the old heart of the city was smashed in 1941. North Road station lies on the north side of the hill. Pennycomequick is a derivation meaning 'at the head of the creek', for in ancient times the inlet we now call Stonehouse Lake came up to where the Post Office depot now stands by the station.

Although the station is on the GWR main line, it was paid for by the London & South Western, to accommodate their trains from 1877 until their own terminus at Friary was ready in 1891. GWR passenger trains used Millbay station until it was abandoned when passenger shipping ceased on the outbreak of war, and it is now used as a carriage depot.

The railway approach to Plymouth is more or less straight down from Hemerdon Siding to the top of the Plym estuary. Here at Tavistock Junction is the principal freight marshalling yard

Left: **On arrival at North Road, you uncouple your engine from the train.** *C. J. Austin*

Above right: **You leave the engine on the coal road at Laira shed. (No 6027** *King Richard I* **on 3 September 1957.)** *P. J. Sharpe*

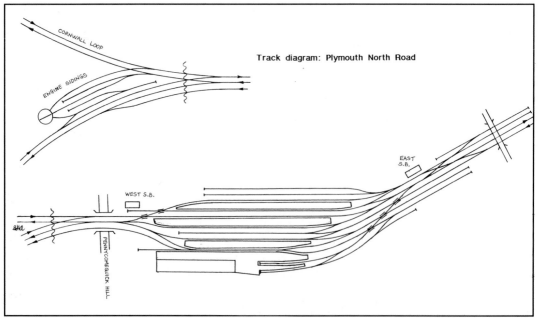

Track diagram: Plymouth North Road

CORNWALL LOOP

ENGINE SIDINGS

EAST S.B.

WEST S.B.

PENNYCOMEQUICK HILL

for the area. Across the river the train runs on the water's edge with a view across to Saltram, the local great house, which has just been taken over by the National Trust. More marshalling and storage sidings lie within the triangular junction at Laira. Under the east end of Laira box is a feature which is at this time unique in Britain, a level crossing of two different gauges. The 4ft 6in gauge Plymouth & Dartmoor Railway was built in 1823, many years before rail links to the rest of the country were contemplated. Far from insignificant among the pioneers, it was the first railway to use a wheel lathe and a mobile crane. Legally it is still open, so the crossing must be maintained, and a wagon is trundled along occasionally to sustain the right of way.

From Laira we turn inland and climb through Lipson Vale, past the site of Mannamead box, through a tunnel under Mutley bowling club and church. Your driver refrains from opening her out on this climb to loosen the fire. Emerging into the wide cutting where Mutley station used to be, a long hiss from No 6849's brake valve is accompanied by a howl from the ATC, as North Road comes into sight. Crossing over to Platform 4, her driver brakes again, lets her run, brakes again and stops at the far end.

Good running up the banks has recovered more time and it is now 3.7pm.

You have made it!

Fortunately you are not on the same platform as the Saltash auto train, awaiting its 3.10 departure, so there is nothing to puncture your euphoria as you drop down the back of the tender to uncouple. The board comes off and you are pulled forward onto the engine sidings by the Millbay branch. Here the pilot is also uncoupled, for No 6849 is going to turn and work

back to Newton Abbot. You check your fire — it looks all right, steam is still on 240lb with half a glass of water — then you sit down to wait while your mate phones the box to tell them who he is and where he wants to go.

Train No 131 has acquired a fresh engine and now departs, followed by the auto train, which as it goes out over Cornwall Loop Viaduct passes a similar equipage coming up. Slowly through the station comes Laira's little saddle tank No 1363, hauling the Navy's supply train from Tavistock Junction to Devonport Dockyard. Not until the 'Cornishman' has appeared does your mate haul himself up the cab steps. 'Take it away, maestro.'

You put her in back gear, blow the brake off, check that the ground signal that lets you out is off, and crack the regulator. You feel proud (not conceited) to be at the helm, taking a curtain call as your engine glides back through the station, making a whistling sound from the front end, and puffs off down the hill. Your mate puts the live steam injector on and gives the fire a pull through, but you know he is only doing it for fun as disposal is not your job. At Lipson Junction the right-hand board is off and you run down the goods loop past the engine shed. Finally you are signalled forward into the yard.

As always there is a line of engines on the pit road, where firedroppers, barmen, ashmen and coalmen are toiling away at the eternal round of mucking out and refuelling iron horses. You ease up to the engine in front, kill the vacuum, open the cylinder cocks, put her in mid gear and screw down the handbrake. Look with satisfaction into the tender from which you have shovelled 5½ tons of coal today. Take your bag from the locker, pack your tea can, and get off the footplate.

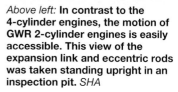

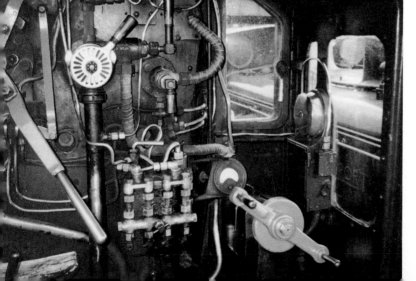

Above left: **In contrast to the 4-cylinder engines, the motion of GWR 2-cylinder engines is easily accessible. This view of the expansion link and eccentric rods was taken standing upright in an inspection pit.** *SHA*

Left: **On the backhead of a No 1 standard boiler. Three steam valves for the injectors, and above them one for train heat. Below them is the regulator gland and jockey arm, and to the right the vacuum gauge and driver's brake valve. This view is on 'Hall' No 6998** *Burton Agnes Hall. SHA*

Below left:
The driver's position on a 'Hall'; a 'Grange' was similar. *SHA*

Above: **A view through the cab window of a 'Hall'. It was taken while the engine was being cleaned, and there is a ladder leaning on the boiler.** *SHA*

Right: **The first 'Grange', No 6800** *Arlington Grange,* **when new; the print is dated 17 September 1936. The location is where most new engine photographs were taken, the southwest corner of A shop at Swindon.** *Great Western Railway*

One and All

While you are waiting for the road back up to Laira, we are about to join the engine which is now backing on to the train. It is another 'Grange', No 6826 *Nannerth Grange*, a name that is not particularly memorable as few people outside the Radnorshire town of Rhayader will have heard of it. At present there are some 530 engines on the Western Region named after piles of masonry; most of them country seats of the gentry whom the Great Western counted as its major supporters, and whose extinction is now proceeding parallel with that of the steam engine. Some of them were close neighbours: Easton had a Court and a Hall, Donnington had a Hall and a Castle, while Broughton in Oxfordshire got a hat-trick with a Hall, a Castle and a Grange. (By the way, for *Walton Grange* you can take your pick from one near Much Wenlock or one north of Clarbeston Road station in Pembrokeshire.)

The 'Grange' is the last-but-one and the best of the various builds to the Churchward 4-6-0 design of 1903. The No 1 standard boiler, brake system, valve motion and frame structure are the same as those of the latter-day 'Saints'. The coupled wheels are standard 5ft 8in units. The new part is the cylinder block. It is basically the Churchward arrangement, two identical castings bolted together along the centre-line, with the main frames attached to the rear of the block, short bar frames attached to the front and the smokebox sitting on top. Cylinder and valve bores are the usual 18½in and 10in, but the upper part has been redesigned with a larger steam chest and wider steam passages. This bigger block is the reason for the raised section in the footplating over the top of it.

The result is an engine which at medium speeds is a better puller than any of the other 2-cylinder 4-6-0s. The crew are certainly happier to have one of these than a 'County', which they dismiss as a goods engine (rightly — it is a larger-wheeled version of the LMS Stanier 2-8-0).

Trains 130 and 635 are normally hauled by 'Castles', of which the star performer for some years has been No 5058 *Earl of Clancarty* and before her, No 111 *Viscount Churchill*, the reconstruction of the erstwhile 4-6-2 *The Great Bear*.

Nannerth Grange was built at Swindon in January 1937 and has spent half her life working from London and half at Penzance. On boarding the footplate, our first impression is of familiarity;

Left: **'Grange' No 6801** *Aylburton Grange,* **painted black with red plates, accelerating the 3.15pm Plymouth-Penzance stopping train over Coombe by Saltash Viaduct on 14 April 1952. In the background is Saltash goods yard.** *R. E. Vincent*

Below: **On the Royal Albert bridge. No 5023** *Brecon Castle* **drifts slowly across with the down 'Cornishman' of 26 May 1956. The circular top flanges to the girders are a Brunel characteristic which may be seen elsewhere, such as on the ship** *Great Britain. R. T. Roxon*

apart from details, the layout is the same as on the 'King' and indeed every other GWR tender engine, even old *City of Truro*. This uniformity is a powerful safety aid. Wherever they are, whatever happens, especially on the dark cold nights which are preferred times for things going wrong, the crew can go for any cab control without hesitating or even thinking about it. The dislike expressed for other engines such as the BR standard types is not prejudice but just the same reaction that Head Office staff would display if someone rearranged the controls of their cars every couple of days.

The main difference from the footplate we have just been on is that she has, as the 'King' did when new, a hydrostatic displacement lubricator in the cab, which the crew can watch and fiddle with, instead of a pump away out on the front end. Some drivers claim that the engines with mechanical pumps do not run so well, but it is difficult to put that down to other than prejudice.

The engine is coupled on and the brake is tested. She has a massive fire almost closing the firehole and the water level is out of sight at the top of the glass. At 3.15 the 'Right-away' is given and under clear signals we move off with a most satisfying bark from our chimney. After working gently across Cornwall Loop Viaduct while the train follows us out, we are into the first bank: 1 in 59 into a deep cutting and through Devonport (Albert Road). The regulator is only open to the first valve and the reverser is left in full forward; in this way we get an even torque on the wheels and the suspended water content of the steam is

slightly reduced. She is shut off through a short tunnel at Albert Road, which is unusual in having another tunnel beneath it: the Plymouth, Devonport & South Western Junction line, down which Southern trains enter Plymouth. The driver then links her up to about 40% and lets her accelerate gradually. At this point we pass the Saltash auto train, two pairs of push-pull coaches with a '6400' class pannier tank in the middle.

On our left the huge sheds and cranes of Devonport Dockyard come into view, while on the right the Southern line can be seen passing round Keyham and Weston Creeks. The two lines come together at the south ends of the otherwise completely separate St Budeaux stations, where a junction was added in 1941 to improve access to the dockyard from the Southern route. The engine blasts up a second bank, a mile at 1 in 62. No wonder they started with a big fire and a full glass. And now, round the bend from St Budeaux appears, like a great artiste commencing our favourite aria, the most beautiful man-made object in England.

There may be bigger structures, grander settings, newer technologies, but nowhere have Science and the Useful Arts composed a sweeter harmony than the Royal Albert Bridge. Her graceful curves match the curves of distant hills upriver; her tracery of ironwork matches the patterns of rigging of the boats below. She frames the river without demeaning it. Her two arms link the great seaport of Plymouth with a Cornish village, Saltash; she reconciles old with new, progress with tradition. She is the beginning, of Cornwall's integration with modern England, and the end, of the creation of the road to the west and of the life of its creator. The image of Brunel taking his first and last look at his completed design from a couch on an open

Above: **Seen from further back, from above Coombe Road, the bridge does not compete with the landscape. Above her is the distant skyline of Dartmoor, with King Tor to the left, over 13 miles away. The 4.20pm Penzance-Newton Abbot, hauled by a 'County', crosses Coombe by Saltash Viaduct, slowing to stop at Saltash. Although it is nearly 7.0pm, the sun is still high on this midsummer day, 25 June 1955.**
R. E. Vincent

Left: **Seen from the Devon side, from Normandy Way, the Saltash 'auto' moves out onto the bridge; about midday on 13 April 1952. The token pick-up post is by the rear coach on the left.**
R. E. Vincent

wagon is the most poignant scene in that long drama.

On a more prosaic note, the bridge we see has been altered over the years, for nothing is truly immutable. Extra cross-members under the track were added in 1903. Brunel's iron side spans were replaced by steel units in 1928, and 10 years later both longitudinals and extra cross-braces were put into the main trusses. The bridge was thus brought up to 'red' load category, which means that it can carry all classes of locomotives except the 'Kings'. Double-headers are permitted, with the exception of a pair of 'Castles', provided that one engine shuts off steam while crossing. A speed limit of 15mph applies. The main trusses and side spans carry but a single track. For the single line section the fireman picks up a tablet from a

post opposite Royal Albert Bridge signalbox and puts it out on a set-down post at the end of Saltash station.

I.K.B. was a consummate artist and he did not neglect to make crossing the Tamar a theatrical experience for the traveller. Before and after, the scene of bridge and river is presented to the train windows, the view, albeit fleeting, from Coombe by Saltash Viaduct being the best of all. In addition, the moment we run off the far end it is clear that we are in another country, for along Saltash platforms are palm trees; the *Cordyline australis*, the insignia of the Cornish Riviera, found on nearly all the immaculately-kept stations from here on.

Our engine slowly rumbles through the arches, with metal spars resonating around us. Waiting in Saltash station is the next up train to cross, the 12 noon Penzance to Crewe mail, which conveys TPO vans and makes a long stop here to load up with letters bound for England. Its steam remains visible for some time as we run down the waterside until we turn inland at the site of Defiance Platform. (HMS *Defiance* was a 'stone frigate' at Wilcove on the far side of the Lynher River.)

The old pre-1908 alignment is visible here in the form of a siding diverging below and left at Wearde box. The main line drives straight on through an enormous cutting, very dull but mercifully short. Before long we are running below the walls of Trematon Castle with a view of the Lynher River winding through its wooded banks. Hereabouts we meet, moving slowly up to Wearde signals, the following up train, and a very important one, the 12.20pm Penzance to Kensington milk. It actually comes up through Cornwall faster than the TPO, although it runs under class C (express freight with vacuum

Above right: **Examples of the posts provided for setting down and picking up single line tokens, with their lamps for night use. This is a set erected at the Didcot Railway Centre, with the Great Western Society workshops in the background.** *SHA*

Below: **At about 11am on Saturday 13 July 1957, the Friday night 11.35pm Liverpool-Penzance accelerates past the overgrown platforms of Defiance Platform; engine No 7925** *Westol Hall*. **The track on the right is on the course of the original line, and now serves as a refuge loop.** *R. E. Vincent*

Above: **St Germans Viaduct, south side, looking upriver.** *K. P. Glanville*

Left: **No 5023** *Brecon Castle* **hauls the down 'Cornish Riviera' through Menheniot station on 16 July 1956, during the period when it did not know whether it was an Express or Limited.** *R. C. Riley*

Below left: **A few minutes later the 12.20pm Penzance-Kensington milk comes through, drifting down the 1 in 80 behind No 6801** *Aylburton Grange.* **Although the train looks very short, each tank wagon weighs 28 tons full and the total load is about 300 tons.** *R. C. Riley*

Above right: **At the east end of Liskeard station, 'County' No 1023** *County of Oxford* **on the 10.40am Paddington-Falmouth slows to stop on Sunday 10 July 1955. As usual, every coach in the train is different, the second one being a 70ft 'toplight'.** *R. C. Riley*

brakes operative on at least half the vehicles). Part of its formation comprises six-wheel tank wagons but there are also several Siphons carrying milk in churns. In 1957 a common sight throughout the West Country is the platform by a farm gate on which churns are placed for the railway lorry to collect.

Our engine did the first two climbs on what she had in the boiler but as she runs over the bridge the live steam injector goes on, for the water is bouncing near the bottom of the glass. The black rear part of the fire is now blazing white. In order to see what is happening further along it the fireman holds his shovel, inverted, just above it and peers underneath. The air stream pulled in by the blast fans the flames out of the way to permit something of a view forward. He throws a succession of shovelfuls down to the front and back up the sides, ending the round by building up the back until once more there is only a narrow gap under the firehole deflector plate. Smoke is rolling out of the chimney all the way down past Wearde. It gradually clears as the driver opens out to full regulator on the climb through the cutting. Steam, which had fallen back to 190lb, rises steadily. Speed rises to about 50mph but falls again as we approach St Germans Viaduct.

St Germans is the viaduct the reader is recommended to choose if only one can be visited; not only is it one of the biggest, it is accessible, which not all Cornish viaducts are, and it has the aesthetic bonus of crossing water. You can walk under it along the west bank of the River Tiddy, and also walk up to enjoy the view from the station's hillside perch. From the footplate we see a sinuous curve through the platforms, and now we are banging away at a steady 30mph up Trerule bank. Coastal views are left behind, the line winds through a patchwork of hedged fields, with just an occasional glimpse of a farmhouse. Turning the top of the bank the engine is eased and starts blowing off, at which firing is resumed. A deep, wooded coombe spreads beneath us: Coldrenick, next to Menheniot station, a twin of St Germans except for having its Brunel chalet building on the down side instead of the up. On the left beyond the station a siding disappears into Clicker Tor Quarry, the railway's principal source of ballast and building stone in Cornwall.

Our ascent continues in the manner to which we are now accustomed. The steady boom of the exhaust in the firebox, with the rattle of the flap-plate and the injector singing under the

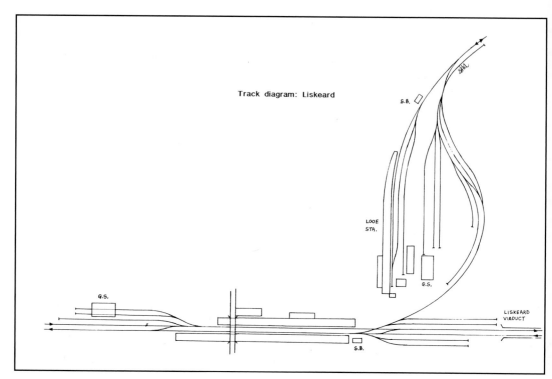

Track diagram: Liskeard

S.B.

LOOE
STA.

G.S.

G.S.

LISKEARD
VIADUCT

S.B.

Left: **A view from the Bolitho road bridge towards Liskeard on 10 July 1955. The goods depot is the nearest range of buildings beyond the deep valley; the booking office is on the skyline to the right of the centre telegraph pole. The train is the Kensington milk again, with engine No 5985** *Mostyn Hall.* R. C. *Riley*

Right: **Looking west from Liskeard station footbridge. No 6879** *Overton Grange* **eases her freight load onto the twisting descent to Moorswater Viaduct. An up freight hauled by a pannier tank has been shunted for an overtaking train.** *M. Mensing*

floor. Occasional swirls of hay or manure smells over the oil and coal dust. The constant thudding of the big ends. Ahead, the rails bending round the next curve, and behind, the long train coming round the last curve.

Cartuther Viaduct is on a down grade, where we ease the engine for the approach to a delightful railway setup that seems too like a model to be true. Looking to the right from Liskeard Viaduct, you see a valley ending in a perfect bowl. A single track, the Looe branch, passes far below, goes round the bowl on a 1 in 40 gradient, and comes back to meet us on the far side. On the skyline are some houses, the edge of the town of Liskeard. Right off the end of the viaduct the station is jammed into an impossible site in two parts, the branch terminus on a hillside and the main line cut through the hill, which is revealed to be a narrow ridge. At the far end the tracks vanish into space.

The explanation of this curious station is that we had here two quite separate railways: the Liskeard & Caradon of 1843, built to bring minerals down from Bodmin Moor to the port of Looe in conjunction with the Liskeard & Looe Canal (later Railway), and the Cornwall on its east-west course, crossing with 200 vertical feet between them. It took 50 years of argufying before work started on a connection, completed in 1901.

Nannerth Grange launches herself into mid-air and we find we are on Moorswater Viaduct, the most airy and vertiginous of the lot, with a panorama of hills all round. Far below on our right appears a toy engine shed, with a toy train beside it: Moorswater depot, the original Liskeard & Caradon terminus.

From the slack over the viaduct we carry on uphill to a summit at Doublebois station. Literally 'two woods' — on the sides of the valley which

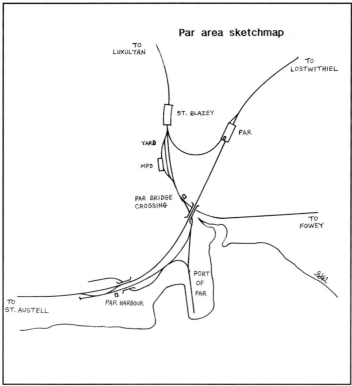

Par area sketchmap

TO LUXULYAN

TO LOSTWITHIEL

ST. BLAZEY

PAR

YARD

MPD

PAR BRIDGE CROSSING

TO FOWEY

PORT OF PAR

TO ST. AUSTELL

PAR HARBOUR

Above: **'County' No 1010** *County of Caernarvon* **struggles up the Fowey Valley with the Saturday 'Royal Duchy', 11.50am Penzance-Paddington, on 25 August 1956. The gradient here is 1 in 70. The centre of the 12-coach train is on the former Draw Wood Viaduct, now filled in.** *P. F. Bowles*

Right: **Truro Viaduct on 19 May 1959. The train departing is the 12 noon Penzance-Glasgow (where it arrives at 7.30 the following morning) hauled by No 6870** *Bodicoat Grange.* **No 7820** *Dinmore Manor* **approaches with a parcels train.** *M. Mensing*

comes in to join us from our right are two distinct tiers of woodland, mostly oak, planted many years ago on the orders of the landowners. A sister 'Grange' with a freight train is waiting in the goods loop round the back of the platform. The reader may recall that the 1.20pm from Tavistock Junction was supposed to precede us from here down to Par but because we have been making up time, it was clear that after 130 had passed it would be impossible for it to go ahead without stopping us, so orders came down from Plymouth to hold it. Its crew look resigned; they will be late getting home to St Blazey, although the overtime payment will be some compensation.

Here the driver shuts down to drifting steam and winds the reverser to about 35% until he obtains a chirruping sound from the chimney, and then takes hold of the brake handle. The river is the Fowey, on its way down from the misty heights of Bodmin Moor to its tranquil deep sea outlet. The train rolls down above the tree-filled valley, curving through woodlands and emerging on viaducts, seven of them in this 4-mile section. Every now and then the brake is needed to keep her down to 45mph.

Bodmin Road station appears, lying on a curve with an even more curved platform road on the right for the branch to Bodmin, which disappears into the trees. A distinctive feature is a water tank on the up side, with a substantial gantry taking the pipe overhead to the platform. It is being used at the moment to water the engine of one of two freight trains which work up through Cornwall in the afternoon: the 3.5pm St Blazey to Tavistock Junction, calling to attach wagons left by the branch freight.

The main line dives away even more steeply, at 1 in 65, from the platform ends. On our right now you may observe large plantations of rhododendrons and formal avenues of very big trees. These are the grounds of Lanhydrock, home of the Robartes family who ruled this district and of whom Thomas Agar-Robartes was a principal in the building of the Cornwall Railway. He had a private drive direct from Bodmin Road station to the house. Now it is open to the public, as the house was donated to the National Trust in 1953. Through a short tunnel and the valley begins to spread out. Above on our right, difficult to see when the leaves are up, is the circular keep of Restormel Castle, well placed to command all approaches to the lowest practical crossing point on the Fowey, at Lostwithiel. It is difficult to realise that the green slopes rising on the other side of the river cover the abandoned workings of the largest iron mine in the West Country.

Left: **A view of Truro Cathedral, at the angle as seen from the train, but taken on 6 July 1996 from a vantage point unavailable in the 1950s: a multi-storey car park.** SHA

The engine is now clattering along quite fast and needs another touch of brake to steady her up. As we sweep grandly round the curve below Restormel, the Dried Milk Products buildings at Lostwithiel come into sight, and beyond them the level crossing and riverside station. Shunting in the dairy is a pannier tank working the second of the up local freight trains, the 3.0pm from St Austell to Laira. The station comprises a range of timber buildings, most unusual for Cornwall. The down yard is full of china clay wagons, recognised by their tarpaulin covers and all-over coating of white, waiting to be worked down to Fowey along the branch line which descends among trees close by the river.

At this point the driver opens her full out in an attempt to keep the speed but on a 1 in 72 we are soon down to slow, heavy slogging. We see something of the long Fowey estuary before turning away across Milltown Viaduct and slogging on past the recently abolished Treverrin box into Treverrin Tunnel. On this bank, as on all of them, our fireman aims to build up his fire at the bottom, so that he does not have to open the flap, admitting cold air, when the draught is strongest, and does not have a lot of gas coming off the coal when the draught ceases at the top of the climb. This carries the risk of a blow-back into the cab, as a precaution against which the driver turns on the blower every time he closes the regulator. Fortunately this engine is steaming well, so there is no need to stop the injector to maintain pressure while climbing; also a risky thing to do. When she tilts her nose down and the regulator is eased, the water level in the rear end of the boiler falls, so it must be kept high enough to allow for this.

Not long into the rush down the other side, the driver makes a prolonged brake application and brings her gently in to a stop at Par station.

Since most expresses stop here, the stranger is surprised to find no urban centre; but Tywardreath, Par and St Blazey are basically large 19th century industrial villages. This was once a rich mining district, developed by the landowner Joseph Austen Treffry, who built the port of Par, a canal to Ponts Mill and a railway up the Luxulyan Valley and over Goss Moor to Newquay. This railway became the Cornwall Minerals Railway and had its headquarters and workshops at St Blazey, which are still in use as a locomotive depot. Under the GWR it developed a large holiday traffic, hence the importance of Par as a junction. Par station feels bleak, as it is one of the few to lack a horticultural display.

Restarting from Par we immediately begin to gain height, so that we have an excellent view from our slowly moving engine of the harbour. The whole area looks dusty rather than dirty, as befits its primary role of shipping china clay and granite. This business has to co-exist with the holiday trade, and it is surprising to visitors from up-country that close on either side of it are the popular beaches of Par Sands and Carlyon.

After about a mile's steady climbing along St Austell Bay, the train turns inland and the sea is obscured behind an area of woodland. Then, still plugging away uphill, we enter a built-up area which is St Austell. As the biggest town in South Cornwall, it is more worthy of a good train service than is Par. However, we do not stop. The station here is frequently photographed, as it has convenient vantage points and is exceptionally pleasant in itself, with a fine display of shrubs, flowers and palms. By now our fireman has to resume firing to keep her going on the long bank, so putting out a massive plume of steam and smoke, not to mention the noise which resounds over the town, she carries on to the summit at Burngullow.

As we rise higher the view to the right opens out to show the famous pure white hills of the clay quarries. China clay is a constituent of a kind of granite which has decomposed. It was discovered at Tregonning Hill, near Helston, by a local explorer William Cookworthy in 1746. Today it is Britain's largest mineral export, at over a million tons a year, half of which goes out on the railway. In this district it is extracted by water jetting. The residue, mostly quartz, is tipped to form the white mounds. The clay slurry is dried in kilns, long low buildings with a chimney at one end and chutes for discharge into wagons alongside. Some of these driers may be seen at Burngullow and on the right of the line at Par Harbour.

Our last view of the clay tips is from Coombe by St Stephen Viaduct. Looking down, it is hard to believe that in the peaceful wooded country just here an unknown Cornish miner's pick unlocked the secret of the most terrifying power in all creation. But so it was, for a mile and a half up the River Fal is Terras, where a mine produced the samples of pitchblende from which Marie Curie discovered radioactivity.

Through the farmland that follows there are only two stations, both set in secluded deep cuttings. Grampound Road has attracted a settlement around it but Probus & Ladock is an unstaffed halt. At about 55mph, *Nannerth Grange* leads her long train down into the Tresillian Valley and drags it up to Polperro. Coming down from Buckshead Tunnel, with Truro spire in sight, the driver puts the brake on, so he is well prepared when the distant signal appears and is on. We drift over Truro Viaduct.

Truro lies at the confluence of two little rivers, the Allen and Kenwyn, which the railway crosses by Truro and Carvedras Viaducts. The view of the town from the train is dominated by the cathedral rising from its centre. The foundation ceremony was in 1880, the main building was completed and consecrated in 1910 and work on the subsidiary structures is still in progress. [Anachronistic note: it was finished in 1967.] It is a fine piece of work, but the impression it makes on this writer is of being squashed into its site, like a model-maker who was determined to have all the traditional features but had not quite

Below: **A footbridge across the whole of Truro station and yard provides a splendid viewing platform. On 18 September 1957, '4500' 2-6-2T No 4574 on an up freight passes pannier tank No 3702. Behind West signalbox are the engine shed and wagon repair workshop.** *P. Q. Treloar*

Left: **The down 'Limited', hauled by a 'Hall', enters Higher Town Tunnel on 13 July 1957.** *R. E. Vincent*

Below left: **Penwithers Junction. The Falmouth line goes straight on and the Newham branch diverges between the signals. No 6808** *Beenham Grange,* **hardly earning her corn, passes on 13 July 1957. Nowadays the Newham branch is a very pleasant public footpath.** *R. E. Vincent*

Right: **A Cornish engine house stands stark and silent in the late evening sun on 7 July 1955. No 1006** *County of Cornwall,* **on an up local train, passes Tincroft Mine near Carn Brea.** *R. C. Riley*

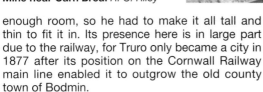

enough room, so he had to make it all tall and thin to fit it in. Its presence here is in large part due to the railway, for Truro only became a city in 1877 after its position on the Cornwall Railway main line enabled it to outgrow the old county town of Bodmin.

The station is in a cramped space between the end of Carvedras Viaduct and a hill. Its buildings are of the standard design which may still be seen all over the GWR from West Ealing downwards. At the far end is found the Falmouth train, held back from its 4.35pm departure to wait for us. Here we pull up, still 10 minutes late at 4.40, and the crew hurry to the rear to water her. The live steam injector and the blower are hard on to keep the fire at high pitch. When he returns to the footplate the fireman stops the injector and moments later, just before we get the right away, the safety valves begin to blow. We start away into a deep cutting and thence to Higher Town Tunnel, which when first used had the distinction of containing two tracks of different gauges. At Penwithers Junction the broad gauge Cornwall line to Falmouth crossed the narrow gauge West Cornwall line to Newham on the level, but after unification the junction was simplified and the Newham branch now leads off the Falmouth line.

Once more *Nannerth Grange* has to go all out up a hill, 3½ miles at 1 in 80, followed by a short drop to Chacewater and a mile and a half at 1 in 65 and 1 in 69 to Wheal Busy Siding. She is expected to average 39mph up this bank, which is not going to happen today. Our driver stands away from the window and flaps his arms, and we know what he means. The regulator is full open, the gear is in full forward, the steam is on the red line, the fireman is pushing coal into her continuously. The only thing we could have to make any difference now would be wings.

This climb takes us into another Cornwall, open, largely bare of trees, covered by abandoned tracks, buildings, waste heaps and rows of houses which would be recognisable anywhere as mining settlements. Most of the detritus left by miners in their short lives has been levelled and nature is reclothing the shattered ground with her kindly shroud of green, but there is ample evidence of the prodigious industry, and indeed of the former prosperity, of the twin towns of Redruth and Camborne.

While we are running through this central region, it might be worth taking time for a history lesson. Personal tastes vary, of course, but to some of us Cornwall is not only beaches but also mining, farming and fishing, and if you do not appreciate that, you cannot know Cornwall. In the mid-19th century this scrap of rock was producing over half the world's copper supply. That could hardly be expected to last; the slump was very hard and from 1870 some 20% of the entire population emigrated. Caradon Hill, employing over 1,500 miners in the 1860s, was deserted by 1910. However, the Camborne School of Mines, founded in 1888, is recognised throughout the world as the leading study centre of its kind, and equipment manufacturers such as Harvey's of Hayle and Holman of Camborne are still world leaders. All the mines are very deep — Dolcoath has levels at 3,300ft down — and were early users of steam power. James Watt worked as Supervisor at Ting Tang Mine in 1777 and Wheal Busy installed the first Watt patent engine in about 1779.

The local agent of the firm of Boulton & Watt, William Murdoch, lived in Redruth and fitted up his house in Cross Street with the first ever domestic gas-lighting. He also constructed the world's first practical self-propelled vehicle. It

Left: **No 1002** *County of Berks* **enters Gwinear Road station from the east on 15 July 1958. Behind the lamp post, the Helston branch disappears through a bridge. On the left can be seen the marshalling yard and East signalbox. The engine is on the wide level crossing immediately at the platform ends.** *MNLPS Collection*

Below: **Hayle had a charming little signalbox on the up platform. At that time, 7 July 1980, the Wharf branch, curving down to the left, was moribund, although it was not formally closed until three years later. The level space is the site of the engine shed.** *SHA*

was what we would call a model, in the proper sense of the word, and he tried it out in his spare time on the paths near his home. It is perhaps only to be expected that this event, whose subsequent impact on the world can hardly be overestimated, is scarcely acknowledged by 'History'. The typically British reaction to it at the time was a stiff letter from his employers forbidding him from indulging in such antics.

Richard Trevithick was a native of Carn Brea and it is rather better recorded that he and three friends were the first people ever to travel on a mechanical vehicle and the first to be carried by steam. That first run, along the road from Camborne to Tehidy on Christmas Eve 1801, had an ignominious sequel four days later when, while they were dining at an inn, the engine ran out of water, became red hot and

Above: **At St Erth on a fine evening. No 6824** *Ashley Grange* **has attached some milk traffic from the Primrose Dairy siding and is returning to her train on the main line.** *P. Q. Treloar*

set fire to the locomotive and the barn where it was parked.

After running slowly round the curve through Redruth, we accelerate past Carn Brea Hill, crowned with its tower which is a monument to Francis Basset, miners' welfare campaigner and supporter of Trevithick. The fireman has now replenished his fire and will put no more coal on. He tidies up all stray coal, cleans the floor and settles down at his ease to take his afternoon tea. From time to time he gives the water gauge a blow-down. Otherwise he watches the road as it descends into more pastoral scenes. Speed is not allowed to rise above about 50mph until after Penponds Viaduct, when the brake is released and his mate elects to steam for a short distance. However, Gwinear Road East signals are on and we stop briefly before drawing forward past the busy yard into the station. Here we stop to provide connection with another branch train, the 5.0pm to Helston, and as before it has been held for our late arrival. It is standing on the single branch road by the wall on our left, three coaches with a '4500' class engine.

Because of a curve in the platform, a leading porter at our end relays the right away to us, and the driver looks back to see the guard hold his green flag from a window to show that he is aboard. This is made more difficult by the arrival alongside of an up train, the Manchester express. The getaway is very fast and we are soon charging down towards another seascape, the North Cornish coast this time. The brake goes on almost at once to prevent things getting out of

hand, holding her down to 45mph on the reverse curves into Hayle. Here we see coming up towards us another train, the 5.5pm express freight from Marazion to Crewe, loaded with fruit, flowers, meat and vegetables. Holiday season is the quiet time for such traffic; during the spring and autumn this engine and crew spend a good deal of their time on extra trains of produce, including the famous broccoli specials.

Through the station, we run onto Hayle Viaduct, low but long, extending above the town centre. Beneath us are the top of the extensive harbour, the original terminus of the Hayle Railway and the buildings of Harvey's, one of the famous Cornish engine builders. Our progress continues down to the meadows and salt marshes of the Hayle River, where more braking is needed. An up grade enables us to make a quick stop in St Erth. It comes as no surprise that there is another branch train waiting. This one is for St Ives; due away at 5.15, it will, like us, be a quarter of an hour late.

The fireman shuts the sliding firedoors and opens the front damper wide for the duration of the start up the rising gradient from St Erth, but then shuts both dampers completely. Steam pressure responds by staying near the red line and then beginning to fall slightly. After only two minutes we are drifting downhill for the last time towards the south coast. Through the window St Michael's Mount is visible, at 250ft overtopping most of the surrounding mainland hills. As we come down towards it the great blue curve of Mounts Bay comes into view.

Nannerth Grange turns her back on the Mount and wheels her happy load of passengers through Marazion. Happy indeed, for they have the apotheosis of the Cornish Riviera before their windows and in a few minutes will be stepping out into it. As the train runs along the foreshore it is flooded with light; the sun is still high, for sun time here is 22 minutes behind Greenwich time.

The driver makes a long brake application so that she slows gradually and steadily, past Ponsandane crossing and through coaches parked on both sides on the up loop and Slopers Sidings. Slower and yet slower, until we are approaching the pointwork outside Penzance station at a fast walking pace, the brakes fading off. She coasts through the points and along the length of Platform 3, close by the coaches of 130 which we last saw when they pulled away from Paddington. Halfway along he puts the brake on again, and with the end of the line getting nearer, a footplate passenger unfamiliar with the time-lag in response of the vacuum brake might experience a moment of alarm. But we are slowing. In sudden dark under the station roof, there is a short burst from the brake ejector — a fine correction. We pull up within a foot of the very end.

It is usual for trains to push back into the sidings, but today the latter are so crowded that ours is to be hauled back to Marazion by a pilot, so we uncouple. We put on the live steam injector to knock her back to 180lb or so, and sit down to wait. The roof over us dates from 1880 but when it was built the edge of the sea wall was located about where the tail of our train is now. Unable to spread on the landward side, the railway was compelled to push out into the water, in 1880, in 1921 and again in 1937. Fortunately the company had the foresight to buy up land further east, between the sea and the main road, where Long Rock locomotive depot was opened in 1914 and Ponsandane goods station in 1937. The plan shows how the facilities are spread along this narrow strip, to within half a mile of Marazion, where there is another large goods station. Our engine is to go into Long Rock for servicing, and to return to Plymouth double-heading with the engine off 130 on the evening mail, whose vans are already in Platform 4.

Now the coaches have gone, we put her into back gear, blow the brake off and trickle her along the platform. Seeing the signal come off, we carry on briskly, cross over to the up line for the mile and a half run, riding on the left side of the cab to wave to people on the sea walk between Ponsandane and Marazion. Arriving at Long Rock box, we see the signalman at his levers. We do not have to tell him our intentions; he promptly pulls off the shunt signal and we move forward into the depot. We run up to the next engine on the coal road and screw her down. Our crew now go off to the mess-room to take their break, while the shedmen replenish the coal and water, clean the fire, refill the lubricator, check the smokebox and ashpan (the way she

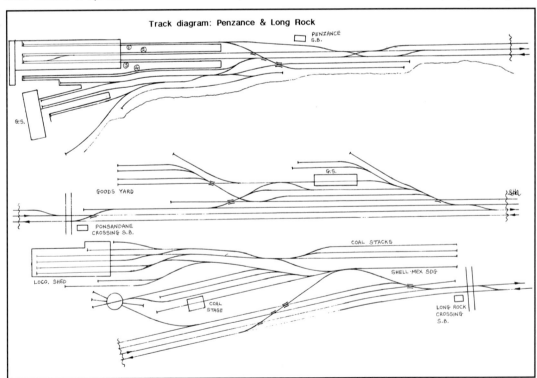

Track diagram: Penzance & Long Rock

Above: **Penzance is one of the most individual of stations, with its backdrop of St Mary's church overlooking the harbour. On the evening of 9 July 1953, Platform 4 contains two trains; No 5023** *Brecon Castle,* **two tanks and a van form the 6.20pm milk train, and the rest of the vehicles are the 7.0pm evening mail.** *C. R. L. Coles*

Below: **Long Rock; No 6875** *Hindford Grange* **passes on the 1.55pm up local. Because Penzance is a terminus and engines are usually turned on arrival on shed, all the engines on Long Rock depot are found facing east.** *M. Mensing*

has been worked, the char didn't have a chance to stay in the smokebox), and turn her. This will take about an hour, then she will be off to the station for the Mail's 7.0pm departure.

By that time we hope our passengers are settling into their rooms, whether in Mount Prospect Hotel (well-appointed) or in 25 Mount Street (homely). But as the sun paints its golden path across the sea, our engine will be on her way again, and she will be crossing the Royal Albert Bridge as Cornwall bathes in its long, warm summer twilight.

Right: **'4500' cab, fireman's side. The coal watering hose is mounted high on the tank side to enable him to put it over the bunker top.** *SHA*

Below: **No 5531 enters the branch station at Liskeard, with the usual train of a 'B' set and an extra coach for summer, on the 9th September 1961. This was the last day of steam on the Looe branch.** *M.L. Roach*

Finale~A Run Down to St Ives

The cult of the Great Western West Country branch line possesses the three principal attributes which a cult should have. It has a wide fan club; goodness knows how many miniature branch lines there are in middle-class bedrooms and attics all over the country. It rests in reality on a narrow base; there are only 12 true branches, or 14 if you add the Teign Valley and Perranporth lines which are through routes, and of those only five serve seaside resorts. And its legitimate owners have no great opinion of it; the Western Region has stated this year that its policy is to close down all branch lines, and local services on main lines, as soon as possible (a process the GWR started in the 1930s).

Of the big five, Brixham is very small and stuck up on a hill, Perranporth is at the back of the town, Looe and Fowey overlook river rather than sea; St Ives is the one with cliffs, beaches, ocean and a full-length express train coming in on Saturdays.

One should not get the wrong idea about St Ives; in fact it is a town three-quarters the size of Penzance and only keeps its reputation for quaintness because the modern development is on high ground out of sight of the harbour. The old part is, though, still picturesque; as a resort it has the advantage of being on a headland with a beach on each side, so if the one turns out to be exposed to the wind, you just pick up your traps and walk over to the other one. The station, also, is not quite what one would expect on a branch line. The platform alone is about 630ft long, and a scale model in the popular 00 gauge will need a length of 20ft if it is to include the little engine shed.

Below: **'4500' 2-6-2T No 4561 of Newton Abbot, standing outside Swindon Works after overhaul on 25 September 1959.** *G. Wheeler*

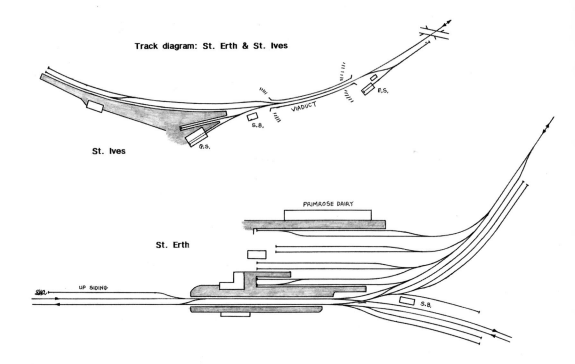

Track diagram: St. Erth & St. Ives

St. Ives

E.S.

VIADUCT

S.B.

G.S.

PRIMROSE DAIRY

St. Erth

UP SIDING

S.B.

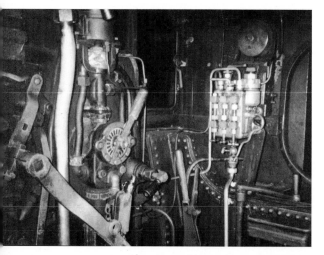

Below: **'4500' cab, driver's side. Note how the reverser lever, hydrostatic lubricator and ATC box are carefully arranged to (unfortunately) prevent the driver from seeing out of the front window.** *SHA*

The branch is 4¼ miles long. The running time for trains is 15 minutes, and as there are no passing loops only one train can be on the move at one time. On a summer Saturday there is little time when the line is not occupied. It starts with a light engine off Long Rock shed at 5.5am, through St Erth at 5.18, arriving St Ives at 5.30; it finishes when the branch train arrives at St Ives

at 10.55pm to stable for the night. There is now no regular freight train, any goods traffic being dealt with by a mixed working each weekday morning, and during the summer the goods shed siding at St Ives is occupied by a camping coach. There is a severe weight restriction; all engines may work into St Erth sidings, but a quarter-mile down the branch stands a notice reading 'Only Uncoloured or Yellow Engines 4500-4574 to pass this Board'. The 4-4-0 '9000' class is also allowed when specially authorised.

On Saturday afternoon the down 'Limited' arrives at St Erth at 5.2pm. It runs through the station and stops at the advance starter signal. Two of the '4500' class engines couple onto it and draw it back over the crossover into the up platform. This has to be done fairly smartly, as the Penzance portion, following down from Truro, is only nine minutes behind. At 5.15 it moves off to the branch.

Our engine will be one of Long Rock's '4500s': as prescribed on the notice, one of the first 75 of the class, as the later ones with larger side tanks are prohibited. A popular one is No 4547, which has the distinction of never being painted in BR black livery. In February 1957 she was overhauled by Newton Abbot Works, repainted green, and now carries a boiler previously used on Taff Vale Railway 0-6-2T No 361. She will start with a good fire in the deep box. The working space for the crew is so

Cab Controls, GWR 2-6-2T engine

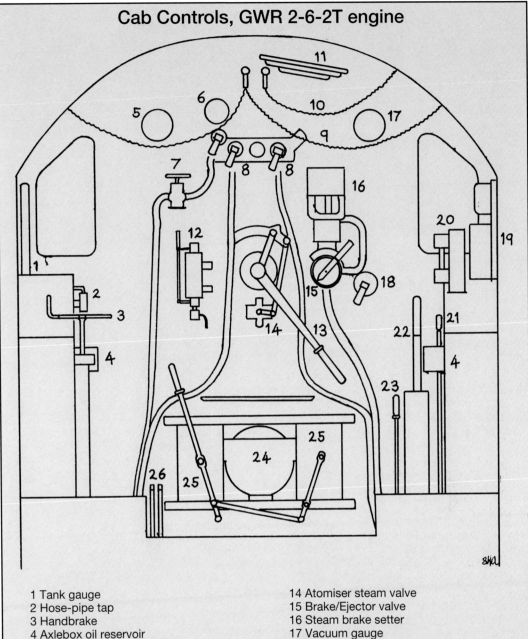

1 Tank gauge	14 Atomiser steam valve
2 Hose-pipe tap	15 Brake/Ejector valve
3 Handbrake	16 Steam brake setter
4 Axlebox oil reservoir	17 Vacuum gauge
5 Boiler pressure gauge	18 Blower
6 Train heat gauge	19 ATC box & bell
7 Train heat control valve	20 Hydrostatic lubricator
8 Injector steam valves	21 Injector water control
9 Whistle pull	22 Reversing lever
10 Alarm whistle pull	23 Cylinder drain cocks
11 Lubricator condenser coil	24 Firedoor flap
12 Boiler water gauge	25 Firedoors
13 Regulator	26 Damper handles

Above: **On the St Ives branch, No 4540 leaves the waterside and heads up to St Erth.**
P. Q. Treloar

Above right: **On Saturday 26 July 1958 the 'Limited' reached St Erth 65min late. It is shown in the down refuge siding, with No 6940 *Didlington Hall* at the far end, and Nos 4547 and 4566 ready to take it onto the branch. The Penzance portion, hauled by No 6911 *Holker Hall*, departs on the main line. The headlamp on the bottom** bracket appears to have been used on the branch when working bunker first. *P. Q. Treloar*

Below: **Nos 4564 and 4571 start away from St Erth with the 10-coach train on 4 July 1959.**
P. Q. Treloar

Right: **Lelant Quay, with the little station nearby. No 4566 with a 'B' set heads for St Ives on 4 June 1960. This engine is now running on the Severn Valley Railway.**
Ian Allan Library

Above: **Carbis Bay, one of the loveliest spots on the Cornish coast. The station is behind the row of houses overlooking the beach, with its booking office above them. Nearer is the 78yd viaduct, overlooking the Carbis Bay Hotel.** *W. R. Rawden*

Above right: **St Ives station and Porthminster beach. The platform extends round the bay to the right-hand edge of the picture. The train is the 11.50am, hauled by No 4570. The massive building above the bridge on the left is the Porthminster Hotel.** *J. C. Beckett*

cramped that her fireman prefers to do his shovelling while stationary, although with this heavy load an extra round halfway through the run may be necessary.

The train drops down through a cutting to the shore and runs along to the old Lelant quay at the mouth of the Hayle estuary. Here the two engines are put to it for a lift at 1 in 60 over Porth Kidney Sands, to a rock cutting through Carrack Gadden. It then runs along the cliff above Carbis Bay, to make a stop in the little platform there. Three minutes are allowed, and possibly exceeded, as it will have to draw up and stop again. Another cutting takes us behind Porthminster Point, and so into St Ives' long station on a ledge above Porthminster Beach. However, when the back of the train is still inside the Point, it stops and the leading engine uncouples and backs into the engine shed siding. The second engine now draws the train into the platform, which is just long enough for its 10 coaches, arrival time being

5.35. The engine which brought in the branch train at 4.55 has shunted its coaches to the run-round loop and retired to the shed. There are thus two engines at the shed, which couple together and come onto the east end of the 'Limited'. At 5.45 the train, now loaded with day trippers leaving the town, moves out. The engine remaining at the west end is not coupled up and, after shoving up the 1 in 60 grade to the Point, drops off and returns to fetch the other coaches. As soon as the 'Limited' has cleared at St Erth, it will haul those coaches back empty.

On arrival at St Erth our train runs straight into the down platform. As soon as the passengers have alighted, it propels back into the down siding in order to clear the way for the 5.30 Truro to Penzance stopping train. The two tank engines leave the coaches there, to be taken down to Penzance by an engine which has come up specially to collect them. With a bit of luck they should get away at about 7.0pm.

Above: **The Saturday morning up through train, the 9.20am, on the bank above Porth Kidney beach, on 4 July 1959; engines No 4564 and No 4571.** *P. Q. Treloar*

Below: **The 'Limited' returning as the 5.45pm from St Ives on 2 August 1958. Nos 4540 and 4547 bring it into St Erth.** *P. Q. Treloar*

Above right: **After delivering its passengers, the train has reversed into the down sidings. This is another view on 4 July 1959, with engines Nos 4564 and 4571 working together. No 6873** *Caradoc Grange* **waits to work it down to Penzance.** *P. Q. Treloar*

Below right: **The two '4500s' move off the coaches to return to the branch.** *P. Q. Treloar*

Below: **The last trip of the day; No 6873** *Caradoc Grange* **draws the empty stock away past Canon's Town. Above the coaches is visible the chimney of the St Erth creamery.** *P. Q. Treloar*

Forty Years On

One should not be too sentimental about the Great Western Railway. Its management achievements included precipitating the General Strike, closing branch lines and substituting buses, and scrapping historic locomotives when other companies were preserving theirs. The Western Region carried on the policy of abandoning branches, and it took a direct order from the Chairman of the British Railways Board to make it desist. Looe and St Ives owe their present train services to that order.

However, there remains an enormous affection for the fabric of the railway. Its self-sufficiency is a major factor in this; everything from pen-nibs to locomotives was made by it or for it, as you realise when you walk into the Didcot Railway Centre. You are not just viewing a collection of items, you are in the Great Western Railway, and one which is in some ways better than the original. It does not occupy Brunel's arches, the South Devon sea wall or the shore of Mounts Bay, but it deserves to.

King Edward II may be seen at Didcot, being rebuilt after years of languishing in a scrapyard. Nothing as big as a complete train of coaches has survived but single examples are available, so you may see in parts the train described in this book. Frome North signalbox is there too,

overlooking an award-winning collection of lineside equipment. Tickets, dining car cutlery — everything we need to reconstruct the 'Limited' is there. This train is, indeed, better preserved in all its aspects than any other, and for that we have the Great Western Society to thank.

The other 'King' which is still running, No 6024 *King Edward I*, was a regular performer on the Plymouth road. You can also see '4500' class engines on the Severn Valley and West Somerset Railways, and pannier tanks — as they should be — all over the place. The great lack is that there is no 'Grange' class engine in existence, showing how survival of artefacts is mainly a matter of chance.

The Cornish Riviera itself is more or less intact, though severely battered; but the superficial popularity of the branch termini has not saved them from destruction. We are not forgetting Kingswear on the Torbay & Dartmouth and Minehead on the West Somerset, for they are both splendid railways, but they were really secondary main lines and will be again. Kingsbridge was nearly saved; Ashburton actually was, until the Government had it suppressed. Although you can reach St Ives and Looe on rails, the present lines bear no resemblance to the originals. If you want to find

Left: **The site of the crossover at the north end of Frome station.** *SHA*

Right: **Forty years on. The site of Frome South signalbox, and the preserved wooden station covering a single line of plain track.** *SHA*

Above: **One of the very few small railway structures to survive east of Exeter was Stoke Canon Crossing signalbox, photographed on 17 July 1994.** *SHA*

Below: **Watering No 5572 on 29 May 1986 outside the engine shed at Didcot, where the Great Western Railway lives on.** *SHA*

the genuine article, you must go to Bodmin. There was precious little left there when rehabilitation started, and it is not near the sea, but it is a complete branch line. The new Bodmin & Wenford Railway also has two other distinctions at the time of writing: it is the only heritage railway with a real junction, and it is the only British railway company of any kind to be running a scheduled freight service in Britain.

There is another branch line, not a complete one at the present time, off the main line in Somerset. The East Somerset Railway, founded in 1855, originally connected Witham with Wells. It is now confined to Cranmore station and a short run westwards, but it has the potential to become an authentic, albeit reconstructed, branch; all it needs is public support.

Any book which tries to draw an 'up to date' conclusion will inevitably be overtaken by events. The writer, who drove the last locomotive to leave Swindon Works under her own steam and was one of the first foreigners to learn of the end of Cornish metal mining, is well aware of the extent of seemingly irrevocable change. The steam train has suffered confident reports of its imminent demise many times since the 'Cornish Riviera Limited' began, but it is still alive. If these pages have given pleasure to those people who like to think back to its past, it is hoped that they will also inspire those who are creating its future.

Left: **Truro East Box was found on 6 July 1996 to be intact. The main station building also survives.** *SHA*